# QUITTING FOR GOOD

## A CHRIST-CENTERED APPROACH

## TO NICOTINE DEPENDENCY

### FRANCES L. MCCLAIN

LIFEWAY PRESS
NASHVILLE, TENNESSEE

# About the Author

**Frances L. McClain** is the former Program Coordinator of the Nicotine Dependence Center at the Mayo Clinic in Rochester, Minnesota. A behavioral therapist and addictions counselor, she has a private practice in Marshfield, Missouri.

**LIFE® Support Group Series Editorial Team**
Betty Hassler, Design Editor
Dale McCleskey, Editor
Kenny Adams, Manuscript Assistant

David Walley, Team Leader/LIFE® Support Group Series Specialist

Illustrations by Doug Jones
Cover Design by Edward Crawford

# Acknowledgements

The writer gratefully acknowledges Richard D. Hurt, M.D., medical director of the Mayo Nicotine Dependence Center in Rochester, Minnesota, without whose mentoring, encouragement, and counsel this work would not have existed.

*Quitting for Good: A Christ-Centered Approach to Nicotine Dependency*
Copyright © 1995 by LifeWay Press

LifeWay Press books are published by The Sunday School Board, 127 Ninth Avenue, North, Nashville, Tennessee 37234

For help for facilitators and leaders in carrying out LIFE® Support Group Series ministries in your church, call 1-615-251-5613.

Item 7200-53    ISBN 0-8054-9943-5    Dewey Decimal Number 613.85
Subject Heading: SMOKING // DRUG ABUSE

Sources for definitions in *Quitting for Good: A Christ-Centered Approach to Nicotine Dependency: Webster's Ninth New Collegiate Dictionary* (Springfield, Mass.: Merriam-Webster Inc., Publishers, 1991).

Unless otherwise indicated, biblical quotations are from the *New American Standard Bible.* © The Lockman Foundation, 1960, 1962, 1963, 1968, 1971, 1972, 1973, 1975, 1977. Used by permission. Other versions used: the Holy Bible, *New International Version,* copyright © 1973, 1978, 1984 by International Bible Society (NIV); the *King James Version* (KJV).

*Printed in the United States of America*

# Table of Contents

# Quitting for Good

## REASON TO QUIT

Mark began to smoke when he was nine years old. For as long as he could remember tobacco had been an important part of his life. At various times he tried to quit. His three children begged him to stop. Through the years several doctors threatened Mark with the health consequences of tobacco use. Nothing really made much of a difference. He made resolutions to cut back. He tried the "Great American Smoke-Out." Always Mark found himself back smoking as much or more than before.

When Mark began to cough more, he switched to smokeless tobacco. He intended to use "spitting tobacco" as a stop-gap measure to help him quit entirely. Instead he found himself just as dependent on snuff as he had been on cigarettes, and he still smoked as well.

When Mark heard about a support group for tobacco users, he was skeptical but he thought: *I'll give it a try. What do I have to lose?*

Many of us can identify with Mark because of the hopelessness that we have felt about our tobacco use. Each year over 430,000 Americans lose their lives due to the health consequences of tobacco use. In 1989 434,00 deaths were caused by active smoking in the United States. More people died from tobacco than the number who died from accidents, AIDS, suicide, homicide, and illegal drugs combined. The magnitude of this loss is even more staggering when you consider the lives of family and friends who grieve these deaths.

Most tobacco users are well aware of the negative effect on health of chronic tobacco use. Like Mark, most smokers say they want to quit using tobacco but find it difficult. The reason is addiction. They are addicted to nicotine.

*Quitting for Good: A Christ-Centered Approach to Nicotine Dependency* could help Mark take some positive steps toward recovering from addiction to nicotine. It would help him realize that rather than being defeated and controlled by the addictive substance, Mark has the power, through Christ, to make decisions that can lead to a nicotine-free life.

The purpose of this material and of *Quitting for Good* support groups is not to wage war against the tobacco industry, battle with social trends, or even promote saved dollars to the health industry. Our one purpose is to offer a way of escape through the power and daily presence of God experienced through Jesus Christ.

On the inside back cover you will find an illustration of the process of recovery from nicotine addiction, which you will study in *Quitting for Good: A Christ-Centered Approach to Nicotine Dependency*. This illustration will help you visualize where you are going on this journey.

*Quitting for Good: A Christ-Centered Approach to Nicotine Dependency* is part of the LIFE® Support Group Series, an educational system of discovery-group and support-group resources for providing Christian ministry and emotional support to individuals in areas of social, emotional, and physical need. These resources deal with such life issues as chemical dependency, codependency, abuse recovery, eating disorders, divorce, and grieving life's losses. Individuals using LIFE® Support Group Series courses will be led through recovery to discipleship and ministry.

*Quitting for Good* is a support-group course designed to be basic to any church's support-group ministry. A support group studies dysfunctional family issues and other life-affecting issues that individuals might face. A carefully selected group facilitator guides discussion of the topics and helps group members process what they have learned during their study. This group is not a therapy group. Rather, this is a self-help group, in which group members help each other by talking in a safe, loving environment.

*Quitting for Good* recognizes that nicotine dependence is a powerful addiction which controls the user physically, psychologically, socially, and spiritually. As you work your recovery program, you will be encouraged to examine your addiction and make changes in each of these four areas. The approach used is one which combines a 12-step chemical dependency process with behavioral changes. You may also want to consult your physician about medications which can minimize withdrawal. By focusing on all three of these areas (withdrawal management, behavioral changes, and chemical dependency actions), you have the best chance of achieving success.

*Quitting for Good* is an integrated course of study. To achieve the full benefit of the educational design, prepare your individual assignments, and participate in the group sessions.

**Study Tips.** Five days a week (which compose a unit) you will be expected to study a segment of content material. You may need from 30 to 60 minutes of study time each day. Even if you find that you can study the material in less time, spread out the study over five days. This will give you more time to apply the truths to your life. Study at your own pace. Study the material as if Fran McClain is sitting at your side helping you learn. When the book asks you a question or gives you an assignment, respond immediately. Each assignment is indented and appears in **boldface type**. When we ask you to respond in writing, a pencil appears beside the assignment. For example, an assignment will look like the one that follows:

✎ **Read Psalm 139:13. Write what the verse tells about God's care for you.**

In an actual activity, a line would appear below each assignment. You would write your answer on this line. When we ask you to respond in a nonwriting manner—for example, by thinking about or praying about a matter—an arrow appears beside the assignment. This type of assignment will look like this:

➤ **Stop and pray, thanking God for being with you during painful times.**

In most cases your "personal tutor" will give you some feedback about your response—for example, a suggestion about what you might have written. Set a definite time and select a quiet place where you can study with little interruption. Memorizing Scripture is an important part of your work.

**Support-Group Session**. Once each week, attend an *Quitting for Good* support-group session designed to help members discuss the content they studied the previous week and share personal responses to issues and problems. These groups provide a safe and loving environment for personal and spiritual healing, growth, and recovery.

The support group adds a needed dimension to your learning. If you are not involved in a group study, try to enlist some friends or associates who also want to stop using tobacco and who will work through this course with you. Approach your church leaders about beginning such a group. *Quitting for Good Facilitator's Guide* provides guidance and learning activities for these sessions. (For orders or inquiries call the Customer Service Center, 1-800-458-2772. Ask for item 7200-54.)

*Quitting for Good* is written with the assumption that you already have received Jesus Christ as your Savior and that you have Him guiding you. If you have not yet made the crucial decision to receive Christ, you will find in unit 2, page 25-26, guidance for how to do so. You will benefit more from *Quitting for Good* if you have Jesus working in and guiding your life. Many people can testify that their relationship with God through Jesus Christ has been the foundation for their recovery. Allow Jesus to work in your life during this time of recovery.

| A key decision |
| --- |

### The Success Story of a Quitter

Anna is a quitter—finally. She smoked for 15 years and was as "hooked" as anyone she knew. Her average was a pack and a half a day, everyday. She started smoking when she was 15 and liked it from the very first puff. What started so innocently graduated to become a nightmare of addiction, guilt, and hopelessness. Anna smoked through both her pregnancies. She smoked in spite of her parents' disapproval and her husband's pleading. Her greatest fear was that she would someday be a "little old lady and still smoking." She also feared she would gain weight if she quit smoking.

Nevertheless, today Anna has been smokefree for an entire year. Her recovery began when a friend asked Anna to join her so they could give up cigarettes together. Anna knew it was impossible for her to ever stop in her own strength, so she prayed. She asked God to give her strength. Then she took it one day at a time. She experienced no magic cure, just a lot of hard work. But Anna says it was worth it. Some of her friends still cannot believe Anna was able to quit smoking, but it's true. Anna is a quitter!

You can join Anna and the thousands of others who give up tobacco each year. You can take the first step right now by saying the following prayer:

> *Father, I admit that I am addicted to nicotine. I know that my hope for recovery lies in You. I surrender my addiction to You and ask that You guide me daily into health and freedom, I am trusting Your strength in this new beginning. Amen.*

# UNIT 1

# Preparing for a Nicotine-free Abundant Life

**Growth Goal:**
You will evaluate your level of nicotine dependence as mild, moderate, or severe and begin laying a foundation of faith for recovery.

## A WEAKENED WITNESS

Kay has never attempted to stop smoking. Since she started, the longest she has ever been without a cigarette is four hours. The very thought of giving up tobacco frightens her. Last week, her Bible study class discussed a passage which stated that the believer's body is the temple of the Holy Spirit. The realization that God is not honored through her tobacco use has been on her mind ever since. She feels that her addiction weakens her witness as a Christian, but she does not know if she can give up her cigarettes.

In this unit you will read about Kay and others like her who have struggled with the need to live nicotine-free lives.

**What you'll learn**

**This week you will—**
- learn about nicotine as an addictive substance;
- identify ways in which your tobacco dependence has robbed you;
- identify the characteristics of nicotine dependence in your life and determine your level of dependence;
- learn that Christ's love and forgiveness is always available;
- consider God as the source of healing from nicotine dependence.

**What you'll study**

| A Prisoner of Nicotine | Counting the Cost | Breaking Free of the Control | Finding Unconditional Love | Accepting Healing from Christ |
|---|---|---|---|---|
| DAY 1 | DAY 2 | DAY 3 | DAY 4 | DAY 5 |

**Memory verse**

**This week's passage of Scripture to memorize—**

*All things are lawful for me, but I will not be mastered by anything.*
—1 Corinthians 6:12

# A Prisoner of Nicotine

Jim smoked his first cigarette when he was five years old. Both his parents and his older brothers smoked, so it was easy to sneak butts from ashtrays. By the time he was nine, he was sneaking whole cigarettes. When he was 13, he began smoking openly. His parents never objected; it was a way of life in the family. Everyone in his family just assumed two things would happen: smoking and heart attacks. Jim's father had his first heart attack when he was 57. His older brothers had theirs when they were 49 and 54. Jim always said that he would stop smoking before he turned 50. So the year before his 50th birthday, he decided it was time. He quit cold turkey and gritted his teeth through three entire days before giving up and smoking one of his wife's cigarettes. In the spring he tried again but relapsed after two weeks. As his birthday approached, he could almost hear the clock ticking.

Jim was highly motivated, partly because of the advice of his doctor who said plainly, "If you want to see your grandchildren grow up, you've got to stop smoking now!" He left the doctor's office with a prescription for a nicotine patch and the telephone number of a nicotine dependence support group. This new information turned out to be exactly what Jim needed. He has now been tobacco-free for 13 months and says he has never felt better. Jim says, "Giving up smoking was one of the most difficult things I have ever done, but it was also the best thing I've ever done for myself and for my family."

**Most difficult/best**

A recent experience reinforced my understanding of how nicotine traps us and how difficult it can be to break free. We have a bird house in our backyard. When my husband and I noticed eggs in the nest, our vigil began. Eventually two of the eggs hatched, and the two little birds began to grow. One bird finally flew out of the nest to begin a life on its own. The second bird stayed in the nest. Each day we expected to find the nest empty; each day the bird lingered.

Pre-Contemplative Stage

When he could stand it no longer, my husband reached down into the nest and pulled the bird out to see if it had some physical problem which prevented its flying away. What he discovered was that a string which the mother had used to make her nest had become tangled around the baby bird's leg—tying it fast to the nest and preventing it from flying away. A snip with a pair of scissors freed the bird's leg. When my husband opened his hand, the baby flew to join its mother who was chirping excitedly.

No plans for abstinence.

✎ **The bird in the story was trapped by a piece of string. Perhaps you identify with the bird. Check any of the following feelings which are true of you.**

- ❑ I feel guilty about my tobacco use.
- ❑ I am afraid of the effect on my health.
- ❑ I know tobacco use hinders my Christian example.
- ❑ I spend money on tobacco which could be spent in better ways.
- ❑ I waste time which could be used more productively.
- ❑ I feel helpless and wonder if I will ever be able to give up tobacco.
- ❑ I realize that my days are scheduled around when I can smoke or use tobacco.
- ❑ Other _____

✎ **In what other ways do you feel trapped by your tobacco use?**

_____

_____

**Guilt, shame, and illness**

Often, nicotine dependence creates guilt, shame, physical illness, and emotional reliance on a substance rather than on the Holy Spirit. It causes you to use financial resources in nonproductive ways. It can deprive you of healthy years spent with a loving family. Nicotine dependence creates a mental preoccupation which enslaves your mind. Answer the following to clarify the hold nicotine dependence has over you.

✎ **List all the places where you purchase tobacco products.**

_____

_____

**How do you normally purchase tobacco?**

❏ By the pack          ❏ One tin/can/pouch at a time
❏ By the carton        ❏ More than one tin/can/pouch at a time

**What brand and type of tobacco do you use?**

_____

**How much tobacco do you use on an average day?**

_____

*God has the power to free you from nicotine dependence.*

Your answers to the above questions indicate how much the use of nicotine controls your daily life. You have rituals or habits as to when and where you purchase tobacco. You have one or two brands you always purchase. The amount of tobacco or number of cigarettes you use each day remains about the same. God has the power to free you from the enslavement of nicotine dependence. God wants to free you. In order to have this abundant freedom, you must place yourself and your addiction in His hands.

✎ **Do you feel tied to tobacco or nicotine?** ❏ **Yes** ❏ **No**

**Do you believe God has the power to free you of your dependence on tobacco?** ❏ **Yes** ❏ **No**

**Do you believe God wants to set you free?** ❏ **Yes** ❏ **No**

➤ **Consider praying the following prayer asking God to help you begin the process that can lead you to freedom.**

*Heavenly Father, I come to You today acknowledging that I am like that small bird—I am trapped in an addiction that holds me in bondage and keeps me from experiencing the fullness of Your abundant life. As I consider making a commitment to stop using tobacco, I ask for Your power this day and a special awareness of Your Spirit's protection and love. Amen.*

✎ **Below write any thoughts or plans you have about your tobacco use. You might write about your reasons for stopping or concerns about your ability to stop. Begin to write a daily journal of your progress.**

_____

_____

_____

_____

All things are lawful for me, but I will not be mastered by anything.
—1 Corinthians 6:12

✎ **Begin to memorize 1 Corinthians 6:12b, your Scripture memory verse for this week. Write the verse on a card to carry with you; practice repeating the verse through the day.**

## DAY 2

**Irene's story**

# Counting the Cost

Irene was 62 before she gave up smoking for good. She started smoking in her teens and continued except for brief periods when she was pregnant with each of her three children. As the children grew, they began to ask her to stop smoking. She always said she knew it was a bad habit and that she would give it up "someday." Irene frequently told herself she was not addicted and could stop smoking anytime she wanted. When her workplace became smoke-free, Irene continued to smoke. Shortly after, she switched to a different brand which she thought might lower her risk of health problems, but she did not stop completely. Her best friend was diagnosed with lung cancer and eventually died, but Irene continued to smoke. When Irene was diagnosed with diabetes, she cut down to 15 cigarettes per day. Actually, her physician told her to give up smoking, but she compromised instead.

Irene found that she could get through the day if she smoked three cigarettes in the morning before work and two or three during her noon break. When her doctor put her in the hospital for a few days because her diabetes was out of control, he suggested it would be a good time for her to stop completely. Irene finally agreed. The smoke-free environment of the hospital and the fact that she was not around anyone using tobacco made it easier than she had thought. The first few days back home were tough, but she has now been tobacco-free for three months and is feeling more confident each day. Irene feels that her ability to remain tobacco-free is related to the time she spends each day reading her Bible and praying.

_You may even feel that tobacco has been a good friend._

Perhaps you are like Irene and think of your tobacco use as simply a habit. You may even feel that tobacco has been a good friend or a part of your personality. The two of you have gone through a lot together—weddings, celebrations, family disagreements, fights with your spouse, anger at your child or boss, times of stress, and even times of grief and loss. Whatever has happened in your life, tobacco was a part of it.

Through the years, you have come to rely on tobacco to get you through the problems and joys of life. It has always been there for you, faithful and true.

It has never talked back to you. It has never caused you grief or worry. It has never betrayed you. It has been with you through thick and thin. Tobacco is your friend. Or is it?

✎ **Is tobacco really a friend? Is it a blessing which is working for good in your life?** ❏ Yes ❏ No

You probably already know that tobacco dependence is a false friend. While appearing to give you self-confidence, relaxation, and energy, it has been robbing you of health, relationships, and self-esteem. Tobacco dependence is not really your friend. It is a thief, the kind of thief described in John 10:10. Tobacco dependence is a thief if it steals from you.

> The thief comes only to steal, and kill, and destroy; I came that they might have life, and might have it abundantly.
> —John 10:10

✎ **Evaluate whether tobacco dependence is stealing any of the following from you. Check the items that addiction to tobacco has taken or is taking from you.**

❏ self-confidence
❏ money
❏ health, the very breath from the body given to you by God
❏ years that you could spend with your family and loved ones
❏ relationships—when you "don't have time" to play with your child because it is your "smoking" time or friendships you did not develop because you avoided nonusers

✎ **How much money have you spent on cigarettes during the past year?**

| | |
|---|---|
| dollars per day | $_____ |
| multiplied by the number of days in a year | x 365 |
| amount you have spent during the year | $_____ |

**Estimate (in today's dollars) how much you have spent on cigarettes during all of the years you have smoked or used.**

number of years you have smoked _____

multiplied by the dollar amount from the exercise above   x $_____

amount in dollars you have spent on tobacco in your lifetime $ _____

**If you had that money in the bank, what could you do with it?**

_____

✎ **Do you or any family members who live with you have any current health problems related to tobacco use? Check all that apply.**

❏ shortness of breath when doing usual activities
❏ shortness of breath when walking fast
❏ cough or phlegm in the mornings
❏ tough places or white patches in your mouth related to smokeless tobacco use
❏ dental problems such as tooth decay or gum disease related to smokeless tobacco
❏ children have more upper respiratory or ear infections than their friends
❏ Other _____

**Do you have any other physical problem which you or your physician think is related to tobacco use?**

_____

_____

Your answers might have made you realize how much tobacco use is costing you both in terms of money and health. When one man stopped smoking, he decided to save the money he had been spending on tobacco. After a period of time, he had saved enough to put a down payment on a vacation cabin.

*Tobacco dependence has also robbed you of control over your body.*

Tobacco dependence has also robbed you of control over your body. Sometimes you smoke or use smokeless tobacco because you need to; your body physically craves the nicotine. It's almost like being hungry, thirsty, or needing a breath of air. You have no control. The need and its accompanying urge are powerful and almost impossible to resist.

The most common time most tobacco users experience this need is first thing in the morning. Most users have their first cigarette or chew within 30 minutes of waking. Some heavy users keep their cigarettes on the nightstand so they can smoke as soon as they open their eyes in the morning, or perhaps even if they wake in the night. Many have a ritualistic way of laying the lighter and cigarettes or tobacco in a specific place on the nightstand. The purpose of all this activity is to have nicotine available and ready to satisfy that first urge of the day. Some who are dependent on smokeless tobacco even sleep with it in their mouth in order to avoid withdrawal.

✎ **How soon after awakening do you smoke or use your first chew?**

❑ within 30 minutes
❑ within an hour
❑ at least two hours after awakening

**Do you have specific places where you put your tobacco when you prepare for bed?   ❑ Yes   ❑ No   Explain your answer**

_____

_____

_____

**What time of day do you most enjoy cigarettes or tobacco? Why?**

_____

_____

_____

**A sign of addiction**

Most professionals in the treatment of nicotine dependence agree that one of the signs of addiction is how soon the person smokes or uses tobacco after waking. If you use within the first 30 minutes, you may be more addicted than the person who waits until the morning work break or even lunch before using tobacco.

**Loss of control**

Another way to examine your physical dependence on nicotine is whether you can control your use. Loss of control over the amount used is a sign of dependence. You may find it difficult to cut down the number of cigarettes or stop using tobacco completely. You may find it difficult to cope with work or social activities where smoking is not convenient or allowed.

✎ **Describe three of your favorite times of day to smoke or use smokeless tobacco.**

_____

_____

**Describe your end of day rituals relating to tobacco.**

_____

_____

**List any of the places you go or activities in which you participate where tobacco is not allowed.**

_____

_____

**Most important moments**

We have looked at the two most important moments of each day, the moment of waking and the moment before going to sleep. Many users will identify the first and last uses of the day as the ones most difficult to give up. Thus, the moments which would ideally be spent with God preparing for a new day or a night of rest are often spent with our addiction.

✎ **Describe the one time you most remember when you ran out of tobacco and did something extreme or out of character in order to get some.**

_____

_____

_____

Be prepared to share the above event in support group this week.

➤ **Take a few minutes to pray. Begin with the following written prayer. Then simply tell God your thoughts and feelings about this process.**

_Thank You, God, for loving me. Thank You for Your faithful self-giving that always desires to bless me. I know You desire only good for my life. I confess today that the ways of the thief are frequently attractive to me and that I sometimes like the easy way out of my problems. Please keep me safe and under Your protection today. Amen._

✎ **In the margin write two or three things you learned about your tobacco use from today's lesson. Write about your hopes or plans for abstinence.**

➤ **Work on memorizing 1 Corinthians 6:12b, this week's Scripture memory passage.**

# Breaking Free of the Control

Kay is 36. She laughingly states that she knows absolutely that she could not survive without her cigarettes. She lights her first cigarette of the day right after she opens her eyes and before her feet hit the floor. She smokes her second while the coffee brews and a third while she is putting on her make-up. She smokes number four immediately after she starts the car and snuffs out number five at the entrance to the office complex where she works. Since she is office manager, she can sneak a smoke here and there throughout the day. When they are especially busy, she skips lunch just taking a few minutes for a couple of cigarettes while standing on the sidewalk.

The best time of day for Kay is the drive home from work when she is alone listening to the radio with her cigarettes. Typically she smokes the last cigarette in the pack right before getting into bed. One of her nighttime rituals is laying a new pack along with her lighter on the nightstand beside her bed.

Kay has never attempted to stop smoking. Since she started, the longest she has ever been without a cigarette is four hours. The very thought of giving up tobacco terrifies her. Last week, her Bible study class discussed the passage in the margin which states that the believer's body is the temple of the Holy Spirit. The realization that her tobacco use dishonors God has been on her mind ever since. She knows that her addiction weakens her witness as a Christian, but she does not know if she can give up cigarettes.

People have different reasons for wanting to stop using tobacco. These include physical, psychological, social, and spiritual reasons. Kay felt that her tobacco dependence was a spiritual problem. She was convicted that she was dishonoring God. As you read today's case story, you might have been able to identify with Kay's feelings. Perhaps you too feel that God is asking you to stop using tobacco. However, not everyone has this feeling. Each individual has personal reasons for wanting to be free of tobacco. You do not need to have the same reasons as someone else.

 **Read the following list of reasons for giving up tobacco. Check all that apply to you.**

❑ physical or health reasons—shortness of breath, physician's advice, tobacco related health problem, family history of health problems related to tobacco use
❑ psychological reasons—feel addicted, loss of pride in myself, ashamed of use
❑ social reasons—inconvenient, changing social acceptance, smoke-free work site
❑ spiritual reasons—harming Christian example, feeling guilty about use

You might have checked only one of the above categories, or you might have checked all of them. Either way is OK. Because you are uniquely created by God, you are distinctly different from all other people. This uniqueness is also seen in how addiction affects you. Why you are giving up tobacco or whether you have one reason or many does not matter. The important issue is to understand the control nicotine has in your life and to be willing to turn to Christ as the answer to your need.

All things are lawful for me, but not all things are profitable. All things are lawful for me, but I will not be mastered by anything.... Or do you not know that your body is a temple of the Holy Spirit who is in you, whom you have from God, and that you are not your own? For you have been bought with a price: therefore glorify God in your body.
—1 Corinthians 6:12, 19-20

## Who or What Is in Control of Your Life?

*You may have learned to depend on nicotine to feel normal.*

Most professionals in the treatment of nicotine dependence agree that nicotine produces addiction in its users. If you have used nicotine to cope with thoughts or feelings over a period of months or years, you may have learned to depend on it to feel normal. For example, if you smoke each time you are stressed, you have learned to depend on smoking to relax.

✎ **Nicotine addiction has definite characteristics. Read the following list of characteristics for nicotine dependence. Check all that are true of you.**

- ❏ I have used nicotine for a longer time than I first intended.
- ❏ I have wanted to stop using tobacco for longer than a year.
- ❏ I have tried one or more times to cut down or stop using tobacco.
- ❏ I spend time buying, organizing, and using tobacco that could be spent more productively in other ways.
- ❏ At times I oversmoke or use too much tobacco and actually feel ill.
- ❏ I find it difficult to cope in places where tobacco use is forbidden.
- ❏ I sometimes crave tobacco in inappropriate places such as church.
- ❏ I smoke around children or others who may be harmed by my secondhand smoke.
- ❏ I have given up or limited important social, occupational, or recreational activities because of nicotine use.
- ❏ I continue to use tobacco despite knowing that it causes or worsens my physical, psychological, or social problems.
- ❏ I need more nicotine to relax or enjoy myself than I used to.
- ❏ I experience withdrawal symptoms when I use less than my usual amount of tobacco.
- ❏ I use tobacco to avoid withdrawal symptoms.

**How many of the above items did you check?** _____

✎ **Describe what you think the number of items you checked shows about your dependence on nicotine.**

_____

_____

You may agree that you are dependent on nicotine. However, you may not be ready to admit that you cannot give up tobacco in your own strength. The following questions will help you review past attempts to break free of the hold of nicotine. Answer prayerfully and honestly.

✎ **In which of the following ways have you attempted to reduce the risk associated with using tobacco? (Check all that apply.)**

- ❏ Switched to a different brand
- ❏ Changed to a filtered cigarette
- ❏ Stopped smoking or chewing in certain places or circumstances
- ❏ Cut down the amount of tobacco used
- ❏ Switched from one form of tobacco to another
- ❏ Smoked less of each cigarette

**How many times have you attempted to give up tobacco?** _____

**What methods did you use in these attempts?**

_____

_____

**How frequently do you run out of tobacco?**

❑ Never          ❑ Sometimes
❑ Rarely         ❑ Frequently

**If "never" or "rarely," how do you prevent running out of tobacco?**

_____

_____

**What does this careful planning reflect about your need for nicotine?**

_____

_____

**Describe three ways tobacco use has negatively impacted your social life or relationships.**

1. _____

2. _____

3. _____

**Who among your family and friends wants you to stop using tobacco?**

_____

_____

**In what ways has tobacco use limited your physical activities or work/school attendance?**

_____

_____

**Have you had an illness or disease which was caused or made worse by tobacco?**

_____

**In what ways has nicotine dependence negatively affected your family life?**

_____

_____

_____

Hopefully you have now evaluated the control tobacco has in your life. It affects your physical, psychological, social, and spiritual health. The hold of nicotine addiction over you may be weak, strong, or somewhere in between. Nicotine dependence may be mild, moderate, or severe.

✎ Circle the word which you think best indicates your dependence on nicotine.

mild          moderate          severe

➤ Spend some time in prayer. Below you will find a suggested prayer. Tell God your thoughts and feelings as you do this difficult work.

*Lord, Your Spirit convicts me today. I acknowledge that I have included You in my sinful humanity rather than letting Your Spirit produce in me the glory You deserve. Thank You for understanding my humanity. I humbly ask Your forgiveness for allowing nicotine to dominate my body and life. Help me understand in a deeper way the meaning of today's Scripture as it relates to my nicotine dependence. Help me to rely on Your strength rather than tobacco to meet the demands of life. Amen.*

✎ Write from memory 1 Corinthians 6:12b, this week's Scripture verse. You may check your work on page 9.

---

## Finding Unconditional Love

### DAY 4

*The scribes and the Pharisees brought a woman caught in adultery, and having set her in the midst, they said to Him [Jesus], "Teacher, this woman has been caught in adultery, in the very act. Now in the law Moses commanded us to stone such women; what then do You say?" And they were saying this, testing Him, in order that they might have grounds for accusing Him. But Jesus stooped down, and with his finger wrote on the ground. But when they persisted in asking Him, He straightened up, and said to them, "He who is without sin among you, let him be the first to throw a stone at her."*

—John 8:3-7

John 8:1-11 tells about a woman caught in the act of adultery who is brought to Jesus. Her accusers did not see her as a person; they saw her only as a prostitute. It never entered their minds to try to help her out of her life of sin. In their condemnation, they did not even mention her name. To them, she was just a problem—a sinner. They gave no thought to forgiving her. Probably this woman had feelings of hopelessness and helplessness. She may have believed she was so far down in sin that there was no way out. Perhaps no one loved her and cared what happened to her. Certainly no one except Jesus came to her defense.

*Certainly no one except Jesus came to her defense.*

Jesus did not see her as just a woman, a prostitute, or a social problem. He saw her as a person. He saw her need for forgiveness and a new beginning. Jesus knew the needs of this woman. He knew that she needed to experience His abundant life. He offered her unconditional love and forgiveness. All she had to do was reach out and take the forgiveness and power He offered.

The woman may have attempted and failed to change her behavior. She may have been unable to forgive herself for her wrong choices. If you are like most tobacco users, this is not the first time you have decided to stop. Most people who are addicted to tobacco make several attempts to stop before they succeed. It is difficult to continue trying to make any life change. No one likes to fail, and sometimes to give up is easier than to continue trying. Some tobacco users come to think of themselves as bad or weak people. They live as if they are of little value. They suffer low self-esteem. Just as with the woman, God can see through your weakness and failure. God loves you. He wants to give you good gifts from the abundance of His blessing.

✎ **Is the decision to give up tobacco difficult for you? Why or why not?**

_____

_____

**Oh no! Not again!**

Bill said he feared that his friends and family would respond with, "Oh no, not again." Pam said she has difficulty forgiving herself for failure to keep her past commitments to abstinence.

Whether you have tried to give up tobacco 5 times in the past, or 20, or even 100, it is time to forgive yourself and move ahead. You actually have benefited from those past attempts. You know quite a lot about what stopping is like. Think about other things you learned to do from the process of trial and error. Were you able to ride a bike the first time you tried? Probably not. Learning is always a process whether you are learning to swim, use a computer, play a musical instrument, read, parent, or whatever.

Whether you succeeded the first time is not important. The important issue is to learn from each unsuccessful attempt. God does not give up on His children. He knows your most secret thoughts and feelings and yet loves you. Don't give up on yourself. Accept God's forgiveness, forgive yourself, and move forward into the abundant life.

Dependence

Dependence

Dependence

Dependence

Dependence

## The Growing Dependence Factor

Another characteristic of addiction is increasing the amount of nicotine used over time. Answer the following questions to understand how your dependence on nicotine has grown.

✎ **When you started using tobacco, how often did you smoke, dip, or chew?**

❑ Daily    ❑ Only on social occasions    ❑ Other

**At what age did you begin using tobacco on a regular daily basis? Describe the circumstances:**

_____

_____

_____

From the time of your very first cigarette or chew, how long was it before you were using your "usual" amount?

_____

Think about any time you were abstinent from tobacco and then relapsed to using it again. How long after you relapsed to using tobacco was it before you were once again using your usual amount?

_____

## Nicotine Withdrawal Symptoms

Most people say that coping with withdrawal symptoms is the most difficult part of giving up nicotine.

✎ **Which of the following withdrawal symptoms have you experienced when you have gone for several hours, an entire day, or longer without nicotine.**

❑ Depressed mood                ❑ Difficulty concentrating
❑ Irritability                  ❑ Decreased heart rate
❑ Frustration or anger          ❑ Changes in sleep pattern
❑ Anxiety                       ❑ Increased appetite or weight gain
❑ Restlessness                  ❑ Other: _____

**How would you describe the above withdrawal symptoms?**

❑ Not bad at all
❑ Bad, but able to stand them for a short while
❑ Unable to stand withdrawal symptoms; relapsed to using tobacco

**What is the longest you have ever been tobacco-free since you began using on a regular daily basis? Explain the circumstances.**

_____

_____

We learn even if we do not reach our ultimate goal. This means you have learned quite a lot about nicotine withdrawal from your past times of abstinence. You have learned ways of coping which helped minimize withdrawal. You have also probably learned some things that did not help reduce withdrawal symptoms.

✎ **What are some ways you have found to cope with withdrawal?**

_____

_____

**What are some ways of coping which did not work for you?**

_____

Now that you have spent time thinking about past periods of abstinence and the severity of your past withdrawal symptoms, you may have decided on the best method of stopping. Next week you will be asked to select a date and a method. We will discuss this more next week, but you should begin thinking now of the method of abstinence you will use.

➤ **Take time to pray about the progress you have been making. You may express the suggested prayer that appears below. Share your thoughts, feelings, and needs with God.**

*Father, I come to You today thanking You for Your unconditional love and forgiveness. Thank You for making it possible for me to be forgiven and to live as a new creation. I ask You to help me forgive myself for my past failures. Thank You for this new beginning. Amen.*

➤ **Below write 1 Corinthians 6:12, your Scripture memory verse for this week. You may check your work on page 7.**

---

---

# DAY 5

## Accepting Healing from Christ

A medical doctor told his story of nicotine addiction and recovery. "Both of my parents were smokers, and I did not like for them to smoke. I experimented a little with smoking during my teens but didn't start smoking regularly until I was 19 or 20. Lots of my friends in college smoked. We had fraternity "smokers" to try to impress and recruit new pledges. At these "smokers," we would have food and entertainment. We hired servers to pass out cigarettes.

"I smoked for three years of college and all four years of medical school. When I was a junior in college, I got sick with **sarcoidosis.** It turned out to be a benign condition but was scary. I asked the doctor if it would hurt my lungs if I continued to smoke. He advised me to stop; I couldn't. In truth, I did not try very hard. I was still young and in denial that anything bad could ever come of it.

"So, I smoked throughout medical school, my internship, duty in the Army, and during my medical residency. When I was doing a research project in an adult drug dependence treatment center, my wife called one day and told me she had signed us both up for a smoking cessation program. I went and stopped smoking November 22, 1975 at 3:30 p.m. It was Saturday, and I was home by myself and scared. There was no such thing as nicotine gum back then to help, so I ate mints. I mean a lot of mints—two or three boxes a day. It was helpful, because it reinforced the fresh smell of my "new" tobacco-free mouth. In my shirt pocket I kept a list of the positives and negatives about tobacco and referred to it many times each day. I also kept a calendar on which I marked off each day I remained smoke-free.

*sarcoidosis* n. a chronic disease of unknown cause that is characterized by the formation of nodules resembling true tubercles esp. in the lymph nodes, lungs, bones, and skin.

Now there is in Jerusalem by the sheep gate a pool, which is called in Hebrew Bethesda, having five porticoes. In these lay a multitude of those who were sick, blind, lame, and withered, [waiting for the moving of the waters; for an angel of the Lord went down at certain seasons into the pool, and stirred up the water; whoever then first, after the stirring up of the water, stepped in was made well from whatever disease with which he was afflicted.] And a certain man was there, who had been thirty-eight years in his sickness. When Jesus saw him lying there, and knew that he had already been a long time in that condition, He said to him, "Do you wish to get well?" The sick man answered Him, "Sir, I have no man to put me into the pool when the water is stirred up, but while I am coming, another steps down before me." Jesus said to him, "Arise, take your pallet, and walk." And immediately the man became well, and took up his pallet and began to walk.

—John 5:2-9

*Sometimes we are comfortable with our addiction or blinded by denial.*

"Over the succeeding weeks living without nicotine became easier, but I still had an occasional urge even a few years later. When my support group was over, I went back as a group facilitator. That really helped. I hope I've passed beyond the stage of risk for tobacco related disease. The ultimate tragedy would be to die of lung cancer!"

John 5:2-9 appearing in the margin tells how Jesus healed a man who had been in bondage. When we read about this miraculous healing, we tend to focus on the day of the miracle—those few minutes when this sick man came face-to-face with Jesus. It is easy to overlook the years of pain and suffering which led to the miraculous deliverance.

The Scriptures do not tell how old this man was, but he had been sick for 38 years. Thirty-eight years! And for at least some period of time, he had been lying at the very edge of the source of healing. He knew he could be healed if he could be the first one to step into the pool after the angel of the Lord came and stirred up the waters. He just never could get there in time. You see, there were so many others who were at the Pool of Bethesda for the same reason. This man was only one among many; and he simply never could quite get there first.

Now this was a wise man. He was in the right place at the right time. This pool was the source of healing—the place of miracles. He even knew the right process for being healed; he had to be the first one into the water at a certain point in time. He had the patience required to wait, day after day. He had the hope that was necessary for healing. He had all of the right answers, but he was still sick.

 Compare John 5:2-9 to your dependence on tobacco. Have you wanted to be healed from your dependence for a long time? For how many years have you wanted to stop using tobacco?

_____

If you were lying on the shore of a miraculous pool into which you could step and be free of your addiction to nicotine, would you step into the water? ❑ Yes ❑ No

This last question might seem ridiculous, but it is the question Christ asked this sick man. Christ asked him, "Do you want to be made well?" The implication is that a sick person might not want to get well. We might prefer to stay dependent on nicotine rather than experience the freedom of recovery. This might be true for many reasons. Sometimes we are comfortable with our addiction, or we may be blinded by denial. We grow fond of our afflictions and weaknesses; they give us fine excuses for not being all we can be. We all know that to continue old patterns is easier than to struggle to change.

The sick man could have refused Christ's offer of healing. He could have chosen to continue to wait for an angel. At times to turn loose of our own plans is difficult—even for a miracle. We have difficulty letting go when we think we know how to cure our own addictions. Because we think we already have the answer, we reject change. Our minds are closed to new understanding, new ways of abstinence, and new relationships. While it is true that no one way of recovery is right for everyone, a common denominator among addicts does exist. We must all give up the thought that recovery can happen according to our plans. We must surrender to God. Only He has the answer to the abundant life of recovery.

✎ **What do you genuinely like about using tobacco?**

_____

_____

**How does smoking or using smokeless tobacco help you cope with emotions and feelings?**

_____

_____

_____

✎ **What will be your biggest challenge in stopping?**

**Your greatest challenge**

_____

_____

_____

**Do you want to be free of your dependence on nicotine? ❏ Yes ❏ No. Explain your answer.**

_____

_____

Although giving up tobacco will be a struggle, John 5:2-9 offers hope when you realize that Jesus Christ is the pool of spiritual healing. You do not need to compete to be the first to be healed. You don't need to push and shove for the grace of God. God's love and mercy extend to all who come to Him in faith.

However, change always involves a cost. To get something from God, you have to give something up. To get closer to God, you must step away from the things that demand your attention and separate you from God. To experience recovery from your nicotine dependence, you will have to give up some things that are comfortable to you. You will have to make adjustments in your life in order to know and find the abundant life God offers.

To gain freedom from your addiction, you will have to experience an inner war between the powerful pull of nicotine dependence and the power of God. Do not underestimate the power of addiction! As you experience healing one-day-at-a-time, pray each day that God will keep you committed to remaining nicotine free.

_God knows how long you have wanted to stop using tobacco._

God knows how long you have wanted to stop using tobacco. He understands how tired you are of struggling. He cares for you. He desires to give you good gifts, and that includes healing from all afflictions, including your dependence on nicotine. The choice is yours.

➢ **Spend some time in prayer. Tell God your thoughts and feelings about quitting, and ask Him to supply the wisdom and strength you need.**

*Father, it would be wonderful today if You would deliver me easily and quickly from the bondage of my nicotine dependence. But I trust You to know what is best for my life. If Your will is that I grow day-by-day, learning to trust in Your power and learning to stop smoking as a process, then I will trust You to give me the daily strength I need. I love You, Lord. I ask for Your healing power to release me from my nicotine dependence and the patience necessary to complete the process, in Your name. Amen.*

## Preparing for Your Support Group Session

Within the next few days, you will meet with your support group of other smokers or smokeless tobacco users who are also in recovery. You can prepare for this session by doing the following.

1. Be prepared to share a brief summary about your use of tobacco. Include how much you use each day, how long you have smoked or used smokeless tobacco, and what happened during previous stop attempts.
2. Be ready to share with the group your reasons for giving up tobacco.
3. Identify the issues or concerns you have about giving up tobacco?
4. Consider the reasons you have to join this support group. What do you hope to gain?

To feel apprehensive at this stage in the recovery process is normal. If you take spiritual steps of faith, this abstinence will be different than your past attempts. You can rely on the power of God rather than on your own strength. You can have the support of a group of persons who are making the same life change and who will encourage you and pray for you.

Next week you will learn about specific methods to give up tobacco. You will select the method that is best for you. If you already know that you want to use nicotine replacement therapy to minimize nicotine withdrawal, contact your physician now to schedule an appointment. Begin thinking about a date within the next two weeks which will become your stop day.

# Understanding and Breaking the Bonds of Nicotine Dependency

**Growth Goal:**
You will plan specific life changes in your spiritual, physical, psychological, and interpersonal health.

## SAM'S STORY

Sam smoked for 20 years, then switched to smokeless tobacco. His uncles on the farm used it, and they didn't seem to have any health consequences. Sam has now been using smokeless tobacco for 15 years. His wife has been telling him for years that it is "disgusting," but he was surprised to learn that his use was related to his tooth decay and gum recession. He also learned that smokeless tobacco use can cause cancer of the mouth and throat, high blood pressure, as well as other health problems. His dentist and his wife both encouraged him to give up smokeless tobacco. This time he's determined not to switch to another form of tobacco but to quit completely. His dentist prescribed a nicotine patch which he's been wearing for the two weeks he's been abstinent from tobacco. Sam knows it's too early to be sure, but he thinks he's going to make it this time.

In this unit you also will identify resources that can help you to make it in your struggle with tobacco.

**This week you will—**

**What you'll learn**
- make a personal decision of faith to begin building the abundant life of recovery;
- decide on the best way of coping with physical withdrawal symptoms during abstinence;
- understand the health risks associated with tobacco use;
- recognize the need to change negative ways of thinking;
- accept the need for support of God, friends, and family during your recovery process.

**What you'll study**

| Tearing Down and Building Up | Choosing a Method | How Tobacco Effects Health | Psychological Health in Recovery | Finding Interpersonal Health |
|---|---|---|---|---|
| DAY 1 | DAY 2 | DAY 3 | DAY 4 | DAY 5 |

**This week's passage of Scripture to memorize—**

**Memory verse** *The thief comes only to steal, and kill, and destroy; I came that they might have life, and might have it abundantly.*

*—John 10:10*

# Tearing Down and Building Up

*I came that they might have life, and might have it abundantly.*

—John 10:10

Turn to the inside back cover of this book. There you will see a course map which illustrates the process of recovery from nicotine addiction. Recovery is a process of individual change. Making the choices and doing the work necessary to become tobacco free is your responsibility. God will provide the strength necessary for you to make those choices and to do that work.

✎ **Review the previous paragraph. Circle God's role in your recovery. Underline your part in your recovery.**

You could have circled "God will provide the strength" and underlined "making the choices and doing the work necessary." You need to understand that depending on God can make this attempt different from previous ones. Your recovery from nicotine dependence will not be an event. It will be a process of faith combined with planning and working. You will live your recovery from nicotine dependence by tearing down your old life of addiction while building a life which is free of tobacco. Each block on the wall of your old life represents a way in which tobacco use formed the pattern of your old life. These blocks represent the reasons you use tobacco.

*Your recovery from nicotine dependence will not be an event.*

✎ **The following activity identifies some of the reasons people use tobacco. Why do you use tobacco? Write one reason in each block; try to use all of the blocks.**

**A wall of addiction**

Your wall of tobacco use represents a wall of addiction. You may have written reasons like *to control weight, to relax,* or *because you enjoy it*. Each of the ideas written above actually is a block in the wall of addiction separating you from abundant life and freedom. You can live free of the need for nicotine. You can tear down this wall of addiction. The first step is admitting that you need Christ to help you build a different life. Your faith in Christ is the foundation on which your abundant life will be built. Faith in Christ is the only secure foundation. By placing your life in His care, you will be laying a secure foundation upon which you can build an everlasting abundant life.

For God so loved the world, that He gave His only begotten Son, that whoever believes in Him should not perish, but have eternal life.

—John 3:16

He who hears My word, and believes Him who sent Me, has eternal life, and does not come into judgment, but has passed out of death into life.

—John 5:24

Knowing this, that our old self was crucified with Him, that our body of sin might be done away with, that we should no longer be slaves to sin; for he who has died is freed from sin.

—Romans 6:6-7

For the wages of sin is death, but the free gift of God is eternal life in Christ Jesus our Lord.

—Romans 6:23

✎ **Match the following truths from Scripture with the appropriate Bible verses appearing in the margin. Write beside each statement the reference of the verse that teaches the truth.**

_____ 1. Because we are all sinners, we deserve the punishment for sin, which is separation from God—eternal death—but because God loves us, He offers us eternal life through Jesus.

_____ 2. Jesus Christ is God's only Son; God gave His Son so that we could have eternal life.

_____ 3. By identifying ourselves with Jesus Christ through repentance and faith, we gain the benefits of His death; because we become *dead to sin*.

_____ 4. When you believe in (trust) Christ, you have eternal life.

**Now go back through the list of Bible teachings. Circle the reference of each that you accept as true.**

All of the above statements are true. The Scripture matches are 1. Romans 6:23; 2. John 3:16; 3. Romans 6:6-7; 4. John 5:24. These and hundreds of other Scripture passages describe God's deep love for you and His desire to have a personal relationship with you. Perhaps you believe the above truths but have never admitted your need for God in your life.

✎ **Has there been a time in your life when you made the decision to accept God's gift of forgiveness and salvation—when you received Jesus Christ as your Savior and Lord?** ❏ Yes ❏ No

If your answer was yes, REJOICE! Your relationship with God can provide the wisdom and strength for victory over nicotine. If your answer was no, thanks for your honesty. If you want to begin the process of life change and growth, you can receive Jesus Christ now by inviting Him into your life.

If you are not 100 percent sure that you would spend eternity with God if you died today and if you are willing to trust Christ and accept His payment for your sin, tell this to God in prayer right now. You may use this sample prayer to express your faith.

*Dear Father, I need You. I want Jesus to be my Savior and my Lord. I accept His death on the cross as payment for my sin, and I now surrender my life to You to love and serve You. Thank You for forgiving me and for giving me a new life. Please help me grow in my understanding of Your love and power so that my life will bring glory and honor to You. Amen.*

_____ (signature) _____ (date)

If you have made Christ the foundation of life, you have the strength, comfort, and guidance of God's Spirit within you. If you made the decision to receive Jesus Christ as your personal Savior, or if you need to discuss the matter further, immediately contact your group facilitator, your pastor, or another Christian that you trust.

✎ **Begin to memorize John 10:10, your Scripture memory verse for this week. Write the verse on a card to carry with you, then practice repeating the verse through the day.**

The thief comes only to steal, and kill, and destroy; I came that they might have life, and might have it abundantly.

—John 10:10

➤ Take a prayer break. Go for a walk and share your thoughts with God. Whether you have made a new commitment to Him, were already committed to Him, or are struggling with your relationship to Him, He cares deeply for you. You can tell Him the truth about your hopes, fears, and doubts.

DAY

2

# Choosing a Method

*But seek first His kingdom and His righteousness; and all these things shall be added to you.*

—Matthew 6:33

**Fran's story**

You read Sam's story on the unit page, page 24. Sam's physical health was his reason to quit. My own reasons for giving up smoking were psychological and spiritual. I wanted to be a good role model to my daughter and the members of my church. I really did not *want* to give up smoking but felt it prevented me from being the example I wanted to be. My reasons for stopping were stronger than my enjoyment. As I look back over the years, I am thankful God led me to abstinence. Because He provided the motivation, stopping was not as difficult as it might have been.

It would be wonderful if recovery from nicotine dependence could be easy for everyone, but the truth is that addiction comes in varying sizes. Compare nicotine dependence to having a rock in your yard. If the rock is small, you can pick it up and throw it away. A medium-sized rock might require a shovel and some effort, but you could move it. But if you have a boulder-sized rock in your yard, you might have to rent a backhoe to get rid of it.

Don't despair if your dependence is a huge "rock." You may even have cause for rejoicing. We all have a tendency to deal with small problems by ourselves and turn to God with the big problems. If you have ever turned to God in a time of desperate need, you know from experience how strong and loving He is. Luke 1:37 says, "nothing will be impossible with God." The bigger your problem, the greater the opportunity for faith. When you know your inadequacy and weakness, you are ready for the power of God to transform your life. As long as you work and struggle in your own strength, you limit God. His power is released when you take that first block of faith and move it into position as the foundation to building an abundant life.

**My dependence is—**

small

medium

large

huge

other _____

✎ **In the margin circle the word which best describes how big you think your dependence on nicotine is.**

Again review the course map inside the back cover. No matter how large or small your addiction, you need God as your source of healing. Your decision to trust God lays the foundation of faith. Once this foundation has been laid, you can build upon it. Your work begins with tearing down the old life of addiction. You will work to remove four types of blocks. They are:

- physical
- psychological
- interpersonal
- spiritual

These four types of blocks represent the characteristics of addiction. Many people fail to realize the need for planning in all four of these areas during recovery. They think they can get up one morning and pitch their pack or can in the trash. They feel like failures when they are digging it out before they finish their morning coffee and back the car out of the garage.

If you really want to stop using tobacco for good, you must develop an adequate plan of action. Think of this plan as a stool with four legs. A stool with four legs offers better balance and support than a stool with three legs. You could sit on a stool with only two legs or even one leg, but you would have to do more work to keep from falling over. In the coming weeks, we will discuss each of these four areas. This week we will take a brief look at all four areas but will focus most on the requirements of physical recovery.

## Physical Recovery

Most tobacco users find that managing physical withdrawal is the first hurdle in becoming nicotine-free. Withdrawal symptoms vary but include craving, irritability, increased appetite, anxiety, difficulty concentrating, restlessness, and decreased heart rate. Some people may experience other symptoms. These symptoms usually become most intense within 24 to 48 hours after the last use and then gradually decrease over the next two weeks. Psychological or interpersonal events, however, also can trigger the urge to use. The effect of these events may be strongest during the first one to several weeks. Thus, the first few weeks are the most crucial. Plan carefully to minimize physical withdrawal symptoms.

## Stop Methods

The most common methods for abstinence are:
- Cold turkey
- Tapering or weaning
- Use of nicotine replacement therapy

**Cold Turkey**
Cold turkey means that you completely stop using all forms of tobacco at a specific point in time. If you have found in the past that physical withdrawal was mild, you might consider stopping cold turkey. If you have not previously stopped using tobacco, you also might consider this method. You cannot know how severe your personal withdrawal will be unless you have experienced it. If you find withdrawal unmanageable, you can revise your stop method later.

**Tapering**
Tapering includes switching to brands lower in nicotine, decreasing the amount of tobacco used, smoking less of each cigarette, or avoiding places in which you smoke or use tobacco. These actions may be effective in changing the psychological habits of smoking, but they may not address physical addiction because they do not reliably reduce the amount of nicotine in the blood stream. An addicted smoker who cuts down on the number of cigarettes will usually inhale more deeply or smoke more of the cigarette. Some persons who switch to brands with lower nicotine levels find they simply smoke more cigarettes or use more tobacco. Thus a person may alter their tobacco use without actually changing the amount of nicotine in the blood stream.

Professionals usually do not recommend trying to taper off tobacco. As long as you continue to use, you reinforce the addiction. As long as you continue to respond to the emotional and environmental cues—such as lighting up when with certain friends—you strengthen the addiction. To taper a little and then set a date to stop altogether may be more effective.

If you choose tapering as a way to prepare for abstinence, you might consider making some changes in the way you smoke for one or two weeks prior to your date for stopping. You might smoke in only one or two locations rather than the many in which you now smoke. This could be a porch, garage, a bathroom, or any other isolated location. It should not be the family room where you smoke while watching television, your favorite chair, the car, the dining room table, or any other of your usual smoking places. Select a location which is somewhat isolated and boring. While you are in your designated smoking area, do nothing else. Just go there, smoke, and leave. Do not read a book, drink a cup of coffee, or chat with anyone. The object is to begin breaking cues, reminders, or situations which you associate with smoking. When you stop smoking, you will find it easier to manage certain situations because you practiced beforehand.

Tapering prior to stopping is not necessary. Some people find it helpful, but others find it only increases their anxiety about quitting. You decide which is best for you. However, do not switch from one form of tobacco to another as a means of tapering. Smokeless tobacco users who wish to taper should consult their physician regarding use of nicotine replacement therapy.

*Smokeless tobacco is related to several medical conditions.*

Some people think smokeless or spitting tobacco is a safe alternative to cigarette smoking, but they are mistaken. The nicotine in spitting tobacco is as addicting as the nicotine in cigarettes. Smokeless tobacco is related to several medical conditions. It raises blood pressure, increases heart rate, narrows blood vessels, is associated with gum recession and tooth decay, and contributes to cancer of the mouth and throat.[1]

### Nicotine replacement therapy

Medications which are useful in treating nicotine withdrawal may be obtained from your physician. These medications include nicotine replacement therapy, available in either gum or skin patch form. Nicotine replacement therapy reduces physical withdrawal symptoms while eliminating the thousands of harmful chemicals contained in tobacco smoke. Nicotine replacement therapy allows the user gradually to reduce the amount of nicotine in the body while totally eliminating the other harmful chemicals and the behaviors associated with tobacco use. This form of nicotine is typically used for up to 12 weeks depending on the intensity of the addiction. If nicotine replacement therapy is not appropriate for you, consult your physician concerning other prescription medications useful in treating nicotine withdrawal.

If you are a very heavy user of tobacco or have certain medical conditions, your physician might run a blood test called a cotinine assay in order to determine the correct initial dosage for your prescription.

➤ **Stop and pray. Ask God's direction as you prepare to stop using tobacco.**

> *Father, I want You to be first in my life. You are more important to me than my tobacco. Help me learn to depend on You to meet all of my needs. Please direct me to the right method of giving up tobacco so that I can experience the fullness of your abundant life, in Your precious name. Amen.*

I am concerned about physical withdrawal because—

_____

_____

_____

✎ Check the method of abstinence which you will use.

❑ cold turkey
❑ tapering
❑ nicotine replacement therapy
❑ other prescription medications

✎ In the margin box write about concerns you have concerning physical withdrawal. Share these concerns with your support group this week.

✎ Repeat John 10:10, your Scripture memory verse for this week.

# DAY 3

# How Tobacco Effects Health

*When He [Jesus] had come down from the mountain, great multitudes followed Him. And behold, a leper came to Him, and bowed down to Him, saying, "Lord, if You are willing, You can make me clean." And He stretched out His hand and touched him, saying, "I am willing; be cleansed." And immediately his leprosy was cleansed.*

—Matthew 8:1-3

The man in this story had a problem. It was a physical problem. In fact, it was the most dreaded disease one could have in Bible times. Leprosy caused increasing disability and eventually death. The diseased person was a social outcast—banished from home, the community, and even the temple. When in a public place, the leper had to cry continually, "Unclean; unclean." This cry was necessary to warn others to keep a safe distance.

What a burden this man brought to Jesus—such pain! His entire life had been destroyed by leprosy. And no cure existed. His disease caused physical, psychological, interpersonal, and spiritual pain. His entire life was being destroyed by this one truth; he was a leper. He was entirely without hope—until he heard about Jesus.

✎ The leper in this passage had an illness which affected his entire life and that of his family. In what ways can you relate to this leper?

_____

_____

_____

**How does your nicotine dependence affect your family?**

_____

_____

**How does your dependence affect your work and social relationships?**

_____

_____

Contemplative Stage

Seriously thinking about abstinence.

As you answered those questions, you may have realized the concern your family members feel when you enter the hospital with tobacco-related health issues. You might have written about the inconvenience of a tobacco-free workplace. You may even feel, as one woman did, that you are viewed by others as a "second class citizen" in a smoke-free society. Admitting your dependence is not easy. You probably have made many efforts to break your dependence. Now it is time to let God do for you what you cannot do alone.

## The Effect of Giving Up Tobacco

Choosing to quit can improve your health. It is never too early or too late to give up tobacco. If you are 16 or 86, abstinence can improve your life. If you are healthy, abstinence can make you healthier. If you already have a disease caused or contributed to by tobacco, stopping now can improve your health.

The Surgeon General's report of 1990 said that smoking cessation has major and immediate health benefits for men and women of all ages. Benefits apply to people with and without smoking-related disease. The following table contains a few of the benefits of abstinence.

✎ **The following table contains the health benefits of smoking cessation stated in the Surgeon General's 1990 report. Read the list carefully. Determine the two benefits you most desire in your life and the two benefits that matter least to you. Circle the benefits you care most about. Draw a line through the benefits you care least about.**

- Former smokers live longer than continuing smokers. For example, people who quit smoking before age 50 have only half the risk of dying in the next 15 years of continuing smokers.
- Smoking cessation decreases the risk of lung cancer, other cancers, heart attack, stroke, and chronic lung disease.
- Women who stop smoking before pregnancy or during the first three to four months of pregnancy reduce their risk of having a low birth weight baby to that of women who never smoked.
- The health benefits of smoking cessation far exceed any risks from the average 5-pound (2.3-kg) weight gain or any adverse psychological effects that may follow quitting.

Sometimes you may be tempted to think, *Well, I've used tobacco so long, the damage is already done.* In fact, stopping has great health and other benefits—no matter how long you have used. You may have circled any two of the benefits. Your reasons for stopping are uniquely your own. You do not have to have the same motivations that others express.

➤ **If you have sometimes felt like the leper in today's study, consider praying the following prayer.**

*Father, I come to You with the same need as this leper. My entire life is affected by my dependence on tobacco. My physical and mental health are made worse. At times, I also feel like a social outcast. I am helpless and without power to heal myself, but I know You are the source of all healing. If You choose, You can make me clean. I ask for this cleansing—not just from my addiction to nicotine—but cleansing of my heart and life as I surrender to You and trust You to work Your will in my life. Amen.*

✎ Describe the most important thing you learned about yourself from the day's study.

_____

_____

➤ Review your Scripture memory verse for this week. Share with God your feelings about the prospect of abundant life—whether those feelings are hopeful, angry, sad, or joyful. Tell God how you are feeling about the prospect of choosing to stop using.

# Psychological Health in Recovery

**DAY 4**

**Seth's story**

*"Are not two sparrows sold for a cent? And yet not one of them will fall to the ground apart from your Father. But the very hairs of your head are all numbered. Therefore do not fear; you are of more value than many sparrows.*
—Matthew 10:29-31

Seth described how he stopped smoking: "The way I gave up cigarettes was something of a miracle. When I became a Christian I knew that both alcohol and cigarettes would have to go. I gave up drinking, but smoking was more difficult. One night I told God that if He did not want me to smoke, He would have to take them away from me because I knew I did not have strength to stop on my own. The next day I went to work as usual but did not smoke a cigarette all day. The second day I carried the same pack in my pocket and again did not smoke. On the evening of the third day, my wife asked, 'Seth, have you quit smoking?' I replied, 'I guess I have.' I then threw away the pack I had been carrying. In all honesty I must say that I did not give up smoking. The Lord just delivered me. I wish it could be that easy for everyone, but I guess it can't. I have learned, though, that asking God for His strength makes every battle easier."

✎ Have you ever wondered why God has not made it easier for you to stop smoking? Do you wish He would just ZAP! you and make your addiction go away? ❑ Yes ❑ No

✎ How do you feel when you hear a testimony like Seth's of how God delivered someone instantly from their addiction?

❑ Skeptical—*I don't believe they were addicted like I am.*
❑ Hopeful—*If it happened for them maybe it can happen for me.*
❑ Angry—*Why them and not me?*
❑ Put down—*Does this mean I'm not worthy of a miracle?*
❑ Other _____

When we read about the miracles Jesus performed, we see only the ending—like scanning a book quickly and rushing to the last page to find out how the story ends. The way God delivered people from their problems just seems so easy, but it was not. The people who received the healing touch of Christ first went through the same human hurts and misery you do. They watched dreams die. They searched for the same goals in life you do.

Take comfort from this truth: you are valuable to God. He knows your struggle. If it is best for you, God can knock down your wall of addiction in one stroke. If that is not best, He will require that you take it down one brick at a time. Whether your wall of addiction comes down quickly or slowly varies from one person to another. After the wall comes down, you can stand around in the rubble, or you can begin the process of recovery.

You are entering a new journey of faith in your walk with Christ. Stopping tobacco usage is a journey of faith which begins with a decision to face the future without the crutch which has supported you for so many years. Beginning this journey takes courage, because you know there will be obstacles. The unexpected will happen, and you will need to make decisions along the way.

*Therefore do not fear; you are of more value than many sparrows.*
—Matthew 10:31

Matthew 10:31 tells us a truth which should give us continuous cause for celebration—we are individually valuable to God. God's love is so great that He carefully watches over all of creation—even little sparrows who were sold two for a penny. Although they are of little value to any human, God knows each time one little sparrow falls to the ground and dies. You are of more value than many sparrows. If God is so concerned with sparrows, how greatly He cares for you! You have nothing to fear—not even addiction. The power you need to be free is found in the abundant resources of Christ.

Recovery is not just a physical process; it is also a process of choice. You will form new ways of thinking. In the weeks ahead, you will learn new ways of dealing with both positive and negative emotions. If God does not take away your addiction instantly like the story that began this lesson, you can choose to reframe the situation. You can look at God's seeming inaction differently. You can see your struggle as God's vote of confidence—as evidence that He knows you can make it and that He considers developing strength of character in your life more important than simply taking the struggle away.

➤ **Pray the following prayer or express your feelings to God in your own words.**

> *Father, I simply cannot comprehend the greatness of Your love for me. Sometimes I think I am hopeless and not worth very much. I don't feel worthy of Your love, but I know You do love me because You said so. I do not understand how Your power can be released only through my weakness. I have so little understanding and such a great need. Please speak to my mind and give me a renewed awareness of Your love for me. I place myself and my addiction into Your caring hands. Thank You for loving me. Help me to love You more. Amen.*

✎ **You can use the following techniques when you doubt your value and feel psychologically stressed. Check the one method you will use today.**

☐ 1. Think: *I am extremely valuable to God. He cares about me.*
☐ 2. Go to bed an hour early each day this week. You will be amazed how much better you can think and cope when you are well rested. Most of us usually do not get enough sleep.
☐ 3. Practice deep breathing when you feel tense. Inhale deeply and slowly. Hold your breath for a few seconds. Then exhale slowly. Do this three or four times while saying, "I am valuable to God."
☐ 4. Use your lunch break to take a walk. Breathe deeply. Look for sparrows, and enjoy the beauty of God's creation.

✎ Reflect on your past as well as the present. In what ways has God demonstrated His protection? How has He shown you that you are valuable to Him?

_____

_____

✎ Write John 10:10 from memory. You may check your work on page 24.

_____

_____

The "thief" mentioned in your Scripture memory verse this week can be tobacco, but the ultimate arch-thief is Satan. He wants you to feel worthless because when you despair, he can control your life.

# Finding Interpersonal Health

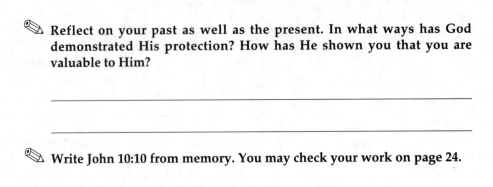

*Come to Me, all who are weary and heavy-laden, and I will give you rest. Take My yoke upon you, and learn from Me, for I am gentle and humble in heart; and you shall find rest for your souls. For My yoke is easy, and My load is light.*

—Matthew 11:28-30

My Dad grew up in the Ozark mountains. When he was young, he plowed with horses named Sam and Daisy. He used a doubletree to hitch the horses and allow them to work together. Daisy was a mare with a hard-working, gentle nature. Sam, on the other hand, was large and lazy. He would lag behind and allow Daisy to do all the work. Sam's behavior did not go unnoticed by my great-grandfather who solved the problem by moving the center balance on the doubletree a few inches closer to Sam. This made Sam pull a greater share of the load.

God gives each of us the responsibility for setting the balance of our spiritual doubletree. In a sense, we are harnessed alongside God, and He allows us individually to set the balance wherever we wish. We can pull the load of life with God pulling half and us pulling half. We can shift the balance so that we carry as much or as little of the burden of life as we desire. God desires that we set the balance so that He carries the burden for us.

✎ How much responsibility does God want for solving the problems in your life?

_____

Why does God say that His yoke is easy and His burden is light?

_____

_____

**doubletree**–n. an apparatus for connecting two horses or mules to pull a plow or wagon

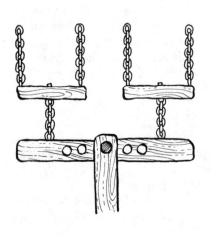

**Does this mean you will not have to work at becoming abstinent from tobacco? Explain.**

_____

_____

The three questions you just struggled with are difficult. God wants us to become responsible. Therefore, just like a good and healthy earthly parent, God gives us tasks to perform. He wants us to become strong, so He does not remove all challenges from our lives. At the same time, God wants us to learn to depend upon Him. Whenever our tasks become a destructive burden, that is a clue that we are depending upon ourselves. We need to learn to allow God to bear the burden for us.

My dad learned that the burden of plowing was easier when shared by two horses. The work went faster when Sam and Daisy worked together rather than individually. The same is true of humans facing many of the responsibilities and challenges of life. God created us with the need for interpersonal relationships. You have people who are significant in your life—family, friends, and co-workers. Sometimes, these special persons also use tobacco.

✎ **In which of the following social events have you smoked or used tobacco with a friend or family member?**

❑ weddings
❑ graduations
❑ movies
❑ drinking coffee with a friend
❑ eating out with a friend or family member
❑ driving on a trip in the car
❑ outside a funeral home
❑ other: _____

Now that you are becoming tobacco free, you may find that being around a person who is using tobacco puts you at risk for relapse. Because you are vulnerable to lapses during the first few weeks of recovery, it is best for you to avoid being around anyone who is not supportive of your commitment. You can either avoid these people, or you can ask for their support. Most friends and family members will agree to help you in any way possible. However, occasionally someone might urge you to give up or unwittingly enable you to use by offering you tobacco. Someone may even sabotage your recovery because they perceive your abstinence as a threat to them.

✎ **Take a few minutes and write a list of all the tobacco users with whom you spend time regularly. Think about persons with whom you live, extended family members, friends, and co-workers. Develop a plan for coping in each of these relationships. Consider telling each person about your commitment to abstinence and asking for their support.**

_____

_____

_____

➤ **Take time to talk with God about the work you have been doing in this lesson. A suggested prayer appears below.**

*God, sometimes I am so angry at life and sometimes even at You. Some things just seem so unfair, and I frequently feel burdened by problems. I release to You each concern of my heart. I trust You to take care of them. Thank You for Your promise to bear my burdens. Thank You that I can always count on Your support. Amen.*

## Making a Covenant to Abstinence

A covenant is a formal binding agreement. Covenants are frequently mentioned in the Bible. People made covenants between individuals, between a leader and people, and between groups or nations. These covenants were made for reasons of securing peace, clarifying trade agreements, affirming friendships, or leaving an inheritance for one's family. The most important type of covenant was not that made between people. It was made between God and people. God made a covenant with Adam, Noah, Abraham, Isaac, Jacob, Levi, and David. In each covenant, God clearly stated what He wanted of the person and frequently gave a blessing which would follow obedience.

After Adam and Eve's sin, God made a covenant with Eve. In Genesis 3:15, God first promised the Messiah or Savior. That covenant was completed with the coming of Jesus Christ and sealed through the giving of the Holy Spirit.

I will put enmity between you [the serpent, Satan] and the woman, and between your seed and her seed; He shall bruise you on the head, and You shall bruise him on the heel.
—Genesis 3:15

Apparently, God thinks there is benefit in having formal agreements or covenants with His people. The covenant clearly stated God's expectations so that the individual, group, or nation did not have to wonder what God wanted of them. It also established that God was going to keep His word in each situation.

From a human standpoint, the covenant gave opportunity to accept or reject God's plan or promise. In each situation, the individual, group, or nation had absolute freedom to say no to God. But if the answer was yes, God expected that humans would keep their promise. We should never take a spiritual covenant lightly. God does not take a covenant lightly.

Speaking from a personal viewpoint, making a covenant places firm boundaries around what I will or will not do. For example, the first time I read my Bible through in a year, I did so because I made a covenant or promise to God that I would do so. Once I had given my word, I worked to keep it.

On the following page, you will be asked to complete and sign a covenant for recovery. It is a spiritual agreement between yourself and God and will not be given to any other person. You will write a date when you will begin recovery. This date is not the end of your recovery; it is the beginning. You will not fully live out your covenant on your stop date. The date you select is only the beginning. You will also clarify your stop method and commit to three actions in the remaining weeks of this support group.

Completing this covenant to recovery from nicotine dependence is more than just signing your name on a piece of paper. It is a spiritual agreement between you and God and may be frightening for you to complete. Remember that although you must make the decision, God is ready, willing, and able to help you live it out. He wants you to succeed. God will not leave you alone to carry out your commitment. In fact, God has already sent His Comforter and Guide to help you. If you have already given your life to God and accepted Jesus as your Savior and Lord, you have the presence of the Holy Spirit around you and within you. The Spirit will be your Helper in the days ahead.

---

*RECOVERY COVENANT*

*I, _____ , commit myself to recovery from my*
                    (name)

*nicotine dependence on _____ .*
                              (type of tobacco used)

*I agree to set a goal for stopping use of all forms of tobacco by_____ .*
                                                              (date)

*The method I will use for stopping will be_____ .*
                    (cold turkey, tapering, nicotine replacement therapy, other)

*I agree to:*
*1. Read the material in this workbook.*
*2. Attend the weekly support group.*
*3. Prayerfully seek God's direction in any and all decisions which I make as part of this program.*

*_____ (Signed) _____ (Date)*

---

## Preparing for the Support Group Session

Be ready to share your answers to these questions.
1. How has nicotine use affected your health?
2. Which of the four dimensions of recovery discussed this week (physical, psychological, interpersonal, spiritual) will be your biggest obstacle in recovery?
3. How motivated are you for abstinence?
4. What stop date and method have you chosen?
5. What concerns do you have about living out the "Recovery Covenant?"

---

Notes

[1]RD Hurt, "The Use of Biochemical Tests in the Management of Patients with Nicotine Dependence", Abstract: American Society of Addiction Medicine, 3rd National Conference on Nicotine Dependence (1990), pg. 39-40.

# Biblical Coping Strategies

**Growth Goal:**
You will make a commitment to abstinence and recovery as well as develop a weekly plan of specific coping methods.

> ### I GOT HELP
>
> "Admitting that I needed help to stop smoking was one of the most difficult things I have ever done. I've been able to do just about anything I set out to do, but cigarettes had a hold on me that seemed impossible to break. Every time I quit smoking and then went back to it, I smoked more than before I had quit. It was a temptation just to give up, but it made me mad that those little white things could control me so easily. One of the guys who works for me joined a smoking cessation group, and he asked me to go along with him. I didn't have a lot to lose, so I went. My original plan was to go for one or two sessions to see what it was all about. Little did I realize it would be just what I needed. Sitting around talking with a group of people who had the same problem I had was a new experience. Each week I'd decide to stay off cigarettes for one more week, and each week I'd go back to the group. When I thought about smoking, I remembered the other people in my group and how difficult it would be to admit my failure to them. Thinking that way worked for me and kept me from giving in. When folks ask me how I quit smoking, I just tell them 'I got help.' "

**What you'll learn**

**This week you will—**
- review and select specific actions which will prepare you for abstinence;
- review methods of abstinence and select one method to use;
- understand choices which deepen spiritual growth;
- identify the struggles of change during abstinence and identify personal high-risk situations;
- understand the role of withdrawal on emotions and review steps for developing Christlike relationships.

**What you'll study**

| Setting Your Face | Managing Physical Withdrawal | Choices and Changes | Building Psychological Health | Building Interpersonal Peace |
|---|---|---|---|---|
| DAY 1 | DAY 2 | DAY 3 | DAY 4 | DAY 5 |

**This week's passage of Scripture to memorize—**

**Memory verse**

*He has made everything appropriate in its time.*

—Ecclesiastes 3:1

# Setting Your Face

*There is an appointed time for everything. And there is a time for every event under heaven—*
*A time to give birth, and a time to die;*
*A time to plant, and a time to uproot what is planted.*
*A time to kill, and a time to heal;*
*A time to tear down, and a time to build up.*
*A time to weep, and a time to laugh;*
*A time to mourn, and a time to dance.*
*He has made everything appropriate in its time.*

–Ecclesiastes 3:1-4,11

**Dale's story**

Dale chose a Saturday to stop using smokeless tobacco. He thought quitting would be easier over a weekend when he was off work and felt less stressed. He chose to use a nicotine patch for four weeks, and his physician set up a plan which put him on a lower dose after two weeks. On his first day without tobacco, he got up and put on his patch first thing. His wife, Martha, cooked breakfast to help him get off to a good start; she also said it was a celebration. During the morning, Dale worked around the house on some projects he had been putting off, and he and Martha went for a walk in the afternoon. They spent an enjoyable evening with friends who did not use tobacco.

As Dale prepared for bed the evening of his first tobacco-free day, he commented to Martha, "You know, today really wasn't as bad as I thought it might be. I think this patch really helps, and I know keeping busy was important. I'm looking forward to tomorrow. My Bible study group is praying for me, and I promised them a progress report in the morning."

## Change Is Part of Life

Life consists of change. Death follows life. Harvest follows planting. Healing comes after disease. We grieve and laugh, build and tear down, find and lose, keep and throw away. Each season of life has a beauty and purpose of its own. None is exactly like any other. Dale was beginning abstinence. He wanted to do everything possible to make sure he got off to a solid beginning. He made specific changes in the routines of his first day without smokeless tobacco. His wife agreed to help. Their plans were successful, and Dale's first day was far easier than he had thought it would be.

 **Review Dale's story above. Circle each decision and action which made it possible for Dale to withstand the temptation of relapsing before he had even begun.**

Did you note that Dale prepared for abstinence by deciding to stop on a weekend when he would be less stressed and that he also chose to use nicotine replacement therapy to ease withdrawal symptoms? Actions Dale took on his stop day included: keeping busy by working on projects around the house, going for a walk, and spending the evening with friends who do not use tobacco. Each of these were wise choices for Dale and improved his chances of success. Dale also made himself accountable by telling his Bible study group at church of his plans to quit. Fortunately, Dale also has an understanding spouse who got his day started right with a good breakfast.

Preparation Stage

Intending to become abstinent in the next month.

## Setting Your Face Toward Recovery

You are entering a season of change called recovery. You have already taken the first step of recovery by admitting you are dependent on nicotine. You have committed to a tobacco-free life. In a way, you have set your life in a new direction.

Set your mind on the things above, not on the things that are on earth.
　　　　　　　　—Colossians 3:2

...he was deeply distressed and set his mind on delivering Daniel...
　　　　　　　　—Daniel 6:14

...for from the first day that you set your heart on understanding this and on humbling yourself before your God, your words were heard.
　　　　　　　　—Daniel 10:12

✎ **In the Bible** *set* **is a powerful word. Read the verses appearing in the margin. Circle the words that the verses speak of "setting."**

**In the first two verses, you probably circled the word** *mind* **and the word** *heart* **in the third verse. In the context of these verses, describe what you think the word** *set* **means.**

_____

_____

*Set* has many meanings. One is to choose a direction. When you set your face toward recovery from nicotine dependence, you have made a decision to turn your life in a new direction. This new direction is a tobacco-free abundant life of freedom, health, and spiritual strength. Choosing abstinence sets your heart and mind toward an abundant life.

Look at the course map in the back of your book. Before you can begin the abundant life, you must lay a strong foundation. This foundation is one of trust in God. Laying this foundation of faith does not mean you already have all the attitudes, skills, and discipline necessary to complete your recovery. In fact, you may have few, if any, of these attributes. What you do have is God's power available as you take the next step. As you begin recovery based on faith in Christ, you must deliberately tear down the lifestyle which was built on nicotine. The old habits and routines must be destroyed and replaced with new attitudes and choices.

*You must deliberately tear down the lifestyle which was built on nicotine.*

You need to begin tearing down your old life of addiction by setting a stop date for when you will quit using tobacco. If you have not already stopped using tobacco, you are asked some day this week to set a date for stopping. If you will use nicotine replacement therapy to ease withdrawal symptoms, see your doctor and get your prescription filled in advance of your stop date.

✎ **The following are some changes you will want to consider on your first tobacco-free day. Check any which you did or plan to do on your first day without tobacco.**

❑ Get rid of all tobacco products and paraphernalia. This includes lighters, ashtrays, and pipes. Be thorough in your search. Look in old coats, bags, cabinets, and drawers. Either flush the tobacco down the toilet or tear it into pieces too small to pick out of the trash. Do not give them to a friend.
❑ Clean the inside of your car. Get rid of everything associated with tobacco use—even the lighters and ash trays.
❑ Purchase a supply of snacks to use when you have an urge to smoke or chew. These items might include sugarless gum or candy, mints, red hots, licorice, and fresh fruits and vegetables. Straws, cinnamon sticks, or coffee stirrers are helpful if you just want something in your mouth.

**First-day actions**

❑ Have your clothes cleaned. This gets rid of the smell of tobacco and reminds you of your new life.

❑ Drink extra fluids throughout the day, but limit caffeine to your usual amount or less.

❑ Keep busy. Do something that you have been putting off, or work on a hobby.

❑ Do not sit in your usual place while watching TV, reading, or relaxing. Better yet, rearrange all the furniture in your den or living room.

❑ Get extra sleep during your first tobacco-free week. Continue this as long as needed during the first weeks of recovery.

Doing any of these activities will change your routines. These changes will disrupt your usual patterns and help keep your mind off tobacco.

Part of setting your face toward recovery means that you keep working toward your goal no matter what happens. You will have good and bad days. Some days you may feel you have made a lot of progress. On others you may feel that you are getting nowhere. Continue working and rebuilding your life. You have only one goal—keep your face set toward the abundant life of Christ. Live one day at a time. It may have taken you many years to become addicted, and it will take time for you to rebuild your life.

➤ **Take time to pray. A suggested prayer appears below.**

*God, I have put off for so long making this commitment to quit tobacco. I have been unwilling to risk failure and experience the pain of change. But I know in my heart that it is time. Part of me wants to completely turn away from my tobacco dependence, and part of me wants to cling to it. I choose to set my mind and heart toward You. I ask that You give me strength to resist the urges and temptations which could pull me to my old addiction. I freely choose You as the center of my life and will honestly try to turn to You to meet my daily needs. Amen*

 **Begin to memorize Ecclesiastes 3:1, your Scripture memory verse for this week. Write the verse on a card to carry with you. Practice repeating the verse through the day.**

*For everything there is a season, and a time for every matter under heaven.*
*—Ecclesiastes 3:1*

# DAY 2

# Managing Physical Withdrawal

*He has made everything appropriate in its time.*
*—Ecclesiastes 3:11*

Spring is a wonderful season which I anticipate each year. My husband and I go into the yard and poke around in the flower beds to look for any signs of life. We look under last fall's leaves to see if the crocus bulbs are sending up green shoots. The smell of the damp earth being warmed by the sun reminds us that warmer days and green foliage are coming. Soon the flower beds will fill with God's glory as the crocus, forsythia, and iris bloom.

How did all this life come to be in our flower beds? Two things were necessary. One is God. The second is me. God created life and its potential to sur-

**Plants of Abundant Life**

vive hardship. He made each plant capable of reproducing. But I determine the kind of plants I want in my flower beds and yard. What I plant determines the type of plant which will break the soil and grow. If I want crocus, I cannot plant iris bulbs. If I want lilacs, I cannot plant redbuds. The same truth applies to the lifestyle of addiction. If you plant the thoughts and actions of addiction, you will grow plants of consequences in your body, mind, and relationships.

✎ **Look around your spiritual garden. Which of the following best describes your life's garden?**

❑ I am proud of its beauty and productivity.
❑ I need to do a little weeding and hoeing, but basically things look good.
❑ I need to pull up the flourishing plants of addiction.
❑ I need to plow up the ground and start over.
❑ I don't even have a garden plot.

God desires to give each of us a garden called abundant life. He wants our abundant life filled with the blessings of freedom from slavery and a close relationship with Him. The abundant life is a fertile field. God provides the seeds which will sprout and flourish, but it is up to you to do the work.

Before the spiritual seeds can grow and flourish, you have some weeding and hoeing to do. It's spring today as far as your addiction is concerned and time to pull up the plants of nicotine dependence. Then you can plant the spiritual seeds of wisdom, health, and growth in your abundant life.

✎ **Read through the following list and check those changes in thought or action you would like to make as part of the spring planting of recovery from nicotine dependence.**

**Reasons and goals**

❑ breathe better                    ❑ get rid of cough
❑ feel more socially acceptable     ❑ feel closer to God
❑ live longer                       ❑ have more energy
❑ have more free time               ❑ stop feeling like an addict
❑ spend more time with family       ❑ smell better
❑ other: _____

These are some of your reasons for giving up tobacco. Keep these goals in your memory, or write them down to carry with you.

## Using Nicotine Replacement Therapy

Stick with your plan for managing withdrawal. If you are using a nicotine patch or some other nicotine replacement therapy, be sure to follow directions. Do not skip a day even if you are feeling fine and doing great. The only reason to revise your plan would be development of side effects. If you experience symptoms which seem unusual or which you do not understand, contact your physician for instruction.

## Stopping Cold Turkey

If you are using the cold turkey method of abstinence, consider the following suggestions.
   1. Drink extra non-caffeinated fluids to flush nicotine from your body.

2. Increase your physical activity level as approved by your physician.
3. Use oral substitutes as suggested in unit 2.

## Suggestions for Everyone

Making changes in your morning routine provides structure.

 **Consider the following list of suggestions. Circle those you will do.**

1. Get up earlier and take a 30-minute walk or read your Bible.
2. Get up later than usual so that you have to hurry in order to get to work on time. You will not have as much time to miss your old routines.
3. Eat breakfast. This will help stabilize your metabolism and give you energy and alertness. Avoid sugars and high fat foods if you are concerned about weight gain.

**Avoid the cues**

4. Drink fruit juice instead of a second cup of coffee. For many people, coffee or colas are a cue to smoke. If this is true of you, coffee will automatically make you want a cigarette. Drinking nonacidic fruit juice is a good substitute and probably is not a cue for smoking.
5. Drive a different route to work. You will avoid the stoplights and other situations where you light a cigarette out of habit.
6. Remind yourself that the urge to smoke or chew will not last long. The urge usually passes within a few minutes, if you get your mind on something else.
7. Carry an "urge bag." Put raisins, toothpicks, Bible verses, gum, or other items inside. When you feel the urge to use tobacco, reach in the bag and pull out a substitute.
8. Listen to a favorite tape of inspirational music as you drive or while you dress.
9. Others you can think of to add: _____

_____

**Weekly Plan**

Develop a worksheet to plan your week's activities in each of the four areas of change. Write at least one thing you will do each day. You may select any suggestion from today's reading or an activity of your own choice. Be specific; write the activity and the exact time you will do it. It is important to begin small in each area if you are not already disciplined in that area. Do not start with grand plans; make daily small steps of change.

 **On a separate sheet of paper develop your own weekly plan. Use the sample worksheet below as a guide. We have given you a few suggestions for each column. For now, fill in only the "Physical" column.**

|  | Spiritual | Physical | Mental | Interpersonal |
|---|---|---|---|---|
| Monday | • Read Bible and Pray— 6:45-7:00 a.m. | • Apply nicotine patch—7:30 <br> • Walk—noon to 12:30 <br> • Go to bed 30 min. early | • Use deep breathing when stressed <br> • Work on hobby in p.m. | • Call member of support group <br> • Avoid smokers |

> A suggested prayer appears below. Spend some time talking to God about what you are cooperating with Him to accomplish in your life.

*Thank You, God, for the seeds of life and hope you planted in me when I first gave my life to You. I am sorry that the weeds of addiction have choked out some of the blessings You want to give me. I ask Your help in cleaning out my life and planting Your attitudes, skills, and choices. Help me to begin new growth that will give me more time for the positive things of life. Amen.*

✎ Write the Scripture memory verse for this week twice on the lines below.

_____

_____

_____

_____

He has made everything appropriate in its time.

—Ecclesiastes 3:1

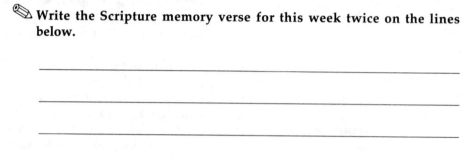

# DAY 3

# Choices and Changes

*On the very night when Herod was about to bring him forward, Peter was sleeping between two soldiers; bound with two chains; and guards in front of the door were watching over the prison.*

—Acts 12:6

**Stan's story**

Stan described his recovery this way: "My addiction to cigarettes was a part of who I was. Smoking ran through me like the core through an apple. When I gave up nicotine, I had a void in the center of my being where smoking used to be. I lived each day feeling as if I had lost some important part of myself. Eventually, I realized that the problem was that I had given up smoking but had not made any other changes. I had to make some difficult choices about changing my old routines. I decided to quit hanging around with my old smoking buddies, and I started exercising. Then I started attending church. These changes did not bring immediate relief, but I felt better about myself. I really don't think I would have made it if I hadn't been willing to change some other parts of my life."

## Faith Is a Choice

Peter's faith was put to the test. He had been arrested by Herod. Herod had abused and even put to death other followers of Christ. Now Peter had been arrested and was to be brought before the people the next day. Peter apparently did not spend his night worrying and doubting God, because we see that he was sleeping. He was sleeping—in prison and bound with chains. In addition, he had soldiers on either side and more stationed outside his cell door. Herod was taking no chances, and Peter's situation looked hopeless. How could Peter sleep under these conditions?

When Peter came to himself, he said, "Now I know for sure that the Lord has sent forth His angel and rescued me from the hand of Herod and from all that the Jewish people were expecting."

–Acts 12:11

Perhaps Peter was able to sleep because he knew there was no way he could solve the problem. He could do nothing except trust in God. When no way of escape existed, Peter took a nap. He made a deliberate choice of faith by deciding to sleep while God solved his problem. While Peter slept, God worked and sent an angel to set him free. Peter must have been in a sound sleep, because the angel had to tell him exactly what to do. The angel told Peter to get dressed, to put on his shoes and coat, and to follow him. Peter did all of this and found himself standing outside. He then "came to himself" (Acts 12:11). Peter woke and realized what was really happening.

✎ **In what ways have you come to yourself concerning your dependence on nicotine?**

_____

_____

✎ **What choices and changes do you know must be part of your recovery?**

_____

_____

## Faith Results in Action

God rescued Peter from a desperate situation in which no way of escape seemed to exist. Once Peter was freed from his bondage, he went right to work. He did not hang around the prison door but began living his freedom in a new way. As part of your recovery, you may need to follow Stan's example in today's case story. You may need to quit hanging around the habits of your former addiction. You can think about how much you enjoyed your old way of life, or you can begin the work of building a new one.

*Peter did not hang around the prison door.*

God also wants to rescue you. He offers you His strength and resources. If you want these resources, you need to spend time with God. You can spend time with God by:
- Reading your Bible every day;
- Praying to God throughout each day;
- Worshipping with other believers;
- Completing the daily workbook assignments;
- Seeing God in His created world.

Action Stage

Becoming abstinent and making life changes to support the commitment.

If the above actions are not already part of your daily discipline, begin with small changes. Spend five or ten minutes reading and praying each day for a week. The second week you can increase the time to 15 minutes. Your goal is to develop spiritual discipline and faithfulness. Follow the same principle as you do with eating. Small daily meals are healthier than one huge meal once a week. Small periods of time alone with God on a daily basis are better than infrequent longer periods of time.

✎ **Look to the weekly plan sheet you created during yesterday's lesson. Complete the section for each day under Spiritual Health. You may choose from the previous suggestions for spiritual growth or use other ideas.**

➤ **Take time to pray.**

*God, I thank You for both the rest and work of life. I realize that I have been lazy in some ways in doing the work of life. Thank You for loving me enough to rescue me through the death of Your Son, Jesus. Instead of keeping my eyes on the physical suffering of these days, give me spiritual eyes to see You at work in my life. I will make You a part of my daily life through Bible reading, prayer, and worship. Amen.*

✎ **Below describe one thing that happened yesterday or today which strengthened your commitment to remaining tobacco free.**

_____

_____

✎ **Below write this week's Scripture memory verse from memory. You can check your work on page 38.**

_____

_____

## DAY 4

**Mike's story**

# Building Psychological Health

"Admitting that I needed help to stop smoking was one of the most difficult things I have ever done. I'm a self-made man. I have built a good life for myself and my family. I own my own business and have worked hard to get where I am today. I've been able to do just about anything I set out to do, but cigarettes had a hold on me that I could not break. Every attempt to quit smoking failed, and I smoked more than before I had quit. I was tempted to give up, but it made me mad that those little white things could control me so easily. A friend joined a smoking cessation group and asked me to go along. I had nothing to lose, so I went with him. I didn't realize it would be just what I needed. Sitting around talking with a group of people who had the same problem I had was a new experience. Each week I'd decide to stay off cigarettes for one more week, and each week I'd go back to the group. When I thought about smoking, I remembered the other people in my group and how difficult it would be to admit my failure to them. Thinking that way worked for me and kept me from giving in. When folks ask me how I quit smoking, I just tell them 'I got help.' "

The Bible tells the following story. Naaman was a commander in the army of Syria, but he suffered from leprosy. A slave girl from Israel said that the prophet Elisha could heal Naaman. So Naaman went to see Elisha, but the prophet did a strange thing. Instead of seeing Naaman personally, Elisha sent a messenger with the message: "Go and wash in the Jordan seven times, and your flesh shall be restored to you and you shall be clean" (2 Kings 5:10).

Naaman became angry at Elisha. He thought the prophet would do something dramatic to cure the disease. He said: "Are not Abanah and Pharpar, the rivers of Damascus, better than all the waters of Israel? Could I not wash

"Had the prophet told you to do some great thing, would you not have done it? How much more then, when he says to you, 'Wash, and be clean'?" So he went down and dipped himself seven times in the Jordan, according to the word of the man of God; and his flesh was restored like the flesh of a little child, and he was clean.

—2 Kings 5:13-14

in them, and be clean?" He was furious. But one of the servants asked the question that appears in the margin.

Naaman was not a man who needed other people. They needed him! But this great soldier was forced to admit that he had an enemy he could not defeat alone. He expected to have a personal appointment with Elisha and was insulted when Elisha sent a message instead of meeting with him face-to-face. Naaman was angry for two reasons. First, he expected that Elisha would meet with him personally and perform a spectacular healing. Second, he thought he knew a better way of healing than Elisha. Elisha told him to go wash in the Jordan River, and Naaman knew the rivers of Damascus were much cleaner than was the Jordan.

Naaman's struggle with pride was not easy. He wanted to be free of his disease and had to decide whether to trust his own intelligence and pride or surrender to God's directing. He finally decided to do as Elisha instructed. The reward for his obedience was healing.

## Recovery Involves Struggle

You too can expect a struggle in your recovery from nicotine dependence. You may want to cling to old behaviors. It may be difficult to admit that you need the help of a medication to manage withdrawal. You may not want to attend a support group. You may not want to admit that you are powerless over your addiction. However, like Naaman, you will have to turn loose of your pride and do some things you don't like in order to gain freedom.

A second part of the psychological struggle with recovery stems from use of tobacco to cope with feelings. Psychological dependence develops when a person uses nicotine to cope with mental and emotional needs. In the early days of recovery when you are learning to live without nicotine, certain feelings or situations may be especially difficult. These circumstances are called "high-risk" situations because during them your mind will urge you to smoke or use tobacco.

 **The following chart lists common high-risk situations. Check those in which you normally use tobacco. Leave the "Plan for Coping" column blank for now. The list is continued on the next page.**

### HIGH-RISK SITUATIONS

| | | Activity | Plan for Coping |
|---|---|---|---|
| ❑ Yes | ❑ No | First thing in morning | _____ |
| ❑ Yes | ❑ No | Around other smokers | _____ |
| ❑ Yes | ❑ No | After meals | _____ |
| ❑ Yes | ❑ No | When relaxing | _____ |
| ❑ Yes | ❑ No | When angry or irritated | _____ |
| ❑ Yes | ❑ No | When bored | _____ |
| ❑ Yes | ❑ No | When stressed | _____ |
| ❑ Yes | ❑ No | When solving a problem | _____ |
| ❑ Yes | ❑ No | When I feel good | _____ |
| ❑ Yes | ❑ No | When nervous | _____ |
| ❑ Yes | ❑ No | When unhappy | _____ |
| ❑ Yes | ❑ No | During/after an argument | _____ |
| ❑ Yes | ❑ No | With coffee or soda | _____ |

❑ Yes ❑ No  Immediately before bed _____
❑ Yes ❑ No  When awake during the night_____
❑ Yes ❑ No  With alcoholic beverages _____
❑ Yes ❑ No  Other: _____

You may have checked yes on one or two items on the list, or you may have checked all of the items. Learning to deal with routine thoughts and feelings without tobacco is a part of recovery. When you feel tense, irritable, anxious, depressed, or even joyful, you will think about smoking or using tobacco. You will miss your old habits for relaxing and coping with stress.

Using mental strategies can help you cope during these early days of being tobacco free. When you experience an urge to use, it helps to get your mind off the urge and onto some other task. You can think about something you need to accomplish, write a grocery list, plan a project you need to do at home, or even sing a song to yourself. You can use some of the following substitutes to cope with these uncomfortable feelings.

✎ **From the following list circle the coping strategies that you think may be helpful for you.**

- Take a few slow deep breaths.
- Take a leisurely walk.
- Talk about your feelings.
- Take a shower.
- Get up from the table.
- Brush your teeth.
- Listen to music.
- Take a nap.
- Read a devotional book.
- Watch a funny movie.
- Call a friend.
- Observe or talk with nonsmokers to discover how they handle feelings and situations.
- Keep a journal of your progress and problems.
- Avoid stressful persons or situations as much as possible.
- Put something besides tobacco in your mouth.
- Do something creative with your hands.

✎ **Now, go back to the High Risk Situations chart on pages 47-48. Use any of the above ways of coping or others you think of to complete the "Plan for Coping" column of the chart.**

A final technique may be useful when all else fails. If you feel that you must give in to the urge, put it off for a few minutes. Tell yourself that you will use tobacco—but later. Then pray, center yourself in God's presence and ask for His strength to resist this urge. Pray and delay for 30 minutes. Usually the urge will go away in a few minutes if resisted. By delaying, you give God a chance to get back in control rather than giving in to addiction.

✎ **Look to the weekly plan sheet you created during day 2. Complete the section for each day under Mental Health. You may choose from the previous suggestions or use other ideas.**

✎ **Write your own prayer in this section.**

_____

_____

<table>
<tr><td>

**DAY**

**5**
</td><td>

# Building Interpersonal Peace

"Let me tell you why I don't care if Larry ever quits smoking or not. He's tried five times, and I remember each one clearly. Larry's not what you would call a nice guy under the best of circumstances. When he's going through withdrawal, he's impossible to live with. The last time he gave up cigarettes, I put up with his anger and verbal abuse for two days. Then I told him he could either smoke or get a divorce; the choice was his. So he went back to smoking. If he ever tries again, I'm leaving."—Larry's wife
</td></tr>
</table>

## Relationships May Produce Stress

*Your body has come to rely on nicotine to feel relaxed.*

Some people have difficulty coping with the demands of relationships and responsibilities of life during the withdrawal period. Your body has come to rely on nicotine to feel relaxed and in control. Withdrawal begins within a few hours after your last use of nicotine. Withdrawal may create changes in your mood. Instead of experiencing your usual range of emotional highs and lows, you may feel edgy and anxious. To respond to others in your usual way may be difficult. You may feel irritable and tense and find yourself saying things that you would not say normally. Even small actions or statements by others may set off a negative response.

Be careful not to use withdrawal as an excuse to be rude and boorish to others. Accept that it may be difficult to cope in spite of your best intentions. Your body and mind will adjust to life without nicotine, but it takes time. After a few days or weeks, you will return to more normal ways of interacting with others. Recognize, however, that if a relationship was not very good to begin with, withdrawal might bring out the worst.

## Coping with Relationships During the Withdrawal Period

Planning ways of coping with these feelings, if they occur with you, can be helpful in avoiding disagreements and arguments.

1. Arrange your schedule so that you have more free time.
2. Communicate honestly with friends, family, and co-workers in advance. Knowing what to expect helps other people alter their actions in order to be supportive.
3. Focus on self-care as much as possible. Get plenty of rest, eat healthy meals, and do things you enjoy.
4. Share your feelings and struggles openly in the support group session. You will learn that many others are experiencing the same problems and having the same challenges.

**Other rewards**

5. Reward yourself for your progress. Smoking or using tobacco has been a powerful reward, and you need to find other rewards to replace it. Some people save the money they would have spent on tobacco products. One couple actually agreed to spend their combined savings to make payments on a vacation cabin. Even small purchases such as a book, bottle of cologne, or shirt can remind you of your progress.
6. If you have someone like Larry's wife in your family or among your close friends, share this relationship with your support group and get feedback for coping.

## Plan for a Weekend Free of Tobacco

*Plan activities which will keep you busy and yet be relaxing.*

The coming weekend will bring changes in the tobacco-free routines you have established thus far. You may have more free time than during the work week, and this can increase the urge to use tobacco. Plan activities which will keep you busy and yet be relaxing. Use the weekend to worship and renew your spiritual focus and catch up on needed rest. Balance these with a pace busy enough to prevent boredom. You might want to clean the closets, straighten the garage, or paint the smoke stained walls in the living room. Whatever your plans, remember to live one day at a time.

 **Add to your weekly plan chart. Fill in the column titled "Interpersonal." This will complete a weekly schedule of activities which comprise your recovery plan. You may use some of the techniques and activities suggested in day 5 to fill out the schedule. Use the weekly plan next week. At the end of next week, evaluate its effectiveness and write a plan for the following week.**

## Preparing for the Support Group Session

Be prepared to share your weekly planning sheet with the members of your group. Questions you may discuss with your group members include:

1. How many days have you been tobacco free?
2. How do you feel about your progress so far?
3. What part of your recovery is going well?
4. In what area(s) are you struggling?
5. What coping methods did you use with good results this week?

Be sure to attend group this week. It does not matter if you have stopped or are still using tobacco. Go to group whether you are finding recovery easy or difficult. Whatever your mood or condition, please attend your weekly group session. If you are doing well, your sharing will help someone else and affirm your recovery. If you are struggling, someone else may lift you up and encourage you. It is too early to trust your feelings, so don't! Make a commitment to faithful group attendance!

# Focusing on Christ to Manage Stress

## AFRAID TO FACE THE STRESS

Glen started using spitting tobacco while in the service. He worked on the flight line, and smoking was strictly forbidden, so he experimented with smokeless tobacco and found he liked it. After discharge, he went to work in a plant where there was a lot of pressure to meet deadlines. The plant was smoke-free, but there were no rules against smokeless tobacco.

Glen developed the pattern of keeping a chew in his mouth most of the time. It helped him stay alert so he could get his job done, and he felt calmer when it was in his mouth. Glen now doubts he could handle his job without smokeless tobacco; it frightens him to even think about it.

In this unit you will examine four resources you can draw upon to manage stress without the aid of tobacco.

**Growth Goal:**
You will continue the process of building an abundant life by learning to manage stress.

**What you'll learn**

**This week you will—**
• define stress, understand its symptoms, and understand how Christ managed it;
• learn five techniques for managing stress and write how each can apply to your needs;
• identify personal problems that abstinence has created and learn the steps of a problem solving method;
• understand how poor time management produces stress and make plans for avoiding personal time-management problems;
• complete a weekly progress check and develop plans for resting over the weekend.

**What you'll study**

| Managing Stress | Using Relaxation Techniques | Solving Problems | Managing Time Wisely | Taking a "Sabbath" Rest |
|---|---|---|---|---|
| DAY 1 | DAY 2 | DAY 3 | DAY 4 | DAY 5 |

**This week's passage of Scripture to memorize—**

**Memory verse**

*After you have suffered for a little while, the God of all grace, who called you to His eternal glory in Christ, will Himself perfect, confirm, strengthen and establish you.*
—1 Peter 5:10

# Managing Stress

*Humble yourselves, therefore, under the mighty hand of God, so that He may exalt you at the proper time, casting all your anxiety on Him, because He cares for you. Be of sober spirit, be on the alert. Your adversary, the devil, prowls about like a roaring lion, seeking someone to devour. But resist him, firm in your faith, knowing that the same experiences of suffering are being accomplished by your brethren who are in the world. And after you have suffered for a little while, the God of all grace, who called you to His eternal glory in Christ, will Himself perfect, confirm, strengthen and establish you.*

—1 Peter 5:6-10

*Don't give up if you haven't stopped yet.*

If you have not yet stopped using tobacco, don't give up. Keep working your recovery program by reading this book and attending group. Every small step of change is a step of progress which moves you in the direction of your goal. Recognize that although you may not have lived through your first day tobacco-free, you are making progress. Don't be discouraged if you struggle or find it difficult to cope with withdrawal symptoms.

 **Circle the phrases in the Scripture above which are actions you could take as part of your recovery. Underline the things God will do for you.**

You might have circled such actions as *humbling yourself, casting your anxiety on God, disciplining yourself, keeping alert,* and *resisting the devil.* God promises He will provide restoration, support, strength, and that He will establish you—make you strong, firm, and steadfast.

**Managing withdrawal**

Managing physical withdrawal symptoms is your most important task this week. If your stop method was cold turkey, you may begin to experience some relief from these symptoms in the near future. Withdrawal differs from person to person, so do not get discouraged if yours lasts longer or is different than some other person's. If you are using nicotine replacement therapy to manage withdrawal symptoms, you have already learned that, although helpful, medications are not magic. Even people who use nicotine patches find they are not receiving the same amount of nicotine from the patch that they did from their tobacco. No matter what medication you are using, you will not feel as comfortable physically as when you were using tobacco.

**Psychological recovery**

Living free of tobacco and the comfortable routines involved with its use is not easy. You had specific reasons for smoking or using tobacco, and these reasons are going to be your personal obstacles to recovery. One reason people use tobacco is to relieve or manage stress. If you fail to learn ways to manage stress other than using tobacco, you will find abstinence difficult.

Nicotine reduces both physical and psychological stress. Before we can learn how to manage stress, we must first understand what it is and how it relates to tobacco use. Many people say that smoking is relaxing and that it calms them down. The act of lighting the cigarette or preparing to use smokeless tobacco creates a mental distraction from the problem at hand. It also offers something concrete to draw attention away from the situation. Each time a person uses tobacco to relieve stress, the link between dealing with emotions and tobacco use becomes stronger. Eventually, any feeling of tenseness or nervousness will trigger the urge to use. Thus tobacco may be used to medicate or deny feelings rather than addressing the problem at hand.

Stress differs from person to person. To break the addictive cycle, you must first identify situations which are personally stressful and examine the emotions which accompany them.

 **Below describe the kind of situation that is stressful for you.**

_____

_____

Stress comes in many forms and differs from one person to another. Stress may be the result of one major event or of many smaller events combined. The real problem of stress, however, is not the actual event but rather how you view that event. One person may find a long car trip stressful while another might look forward to the quiet time away from usual routines. One individual may feel excited and challenged at having many tasks to accomplish while another feels overwhelmed.

## The Body's Response to Stress

Whenever we encounter an unexpected stressful situation, our brains send out messages to our bodies. Our bodies release chemicals which increase our alertness in preparation for taking action. Hormones called adrenaline and noradrenaline are released into the blood stream where they stimulate the heart, raise the blood pressure, and prepare us for a response called "fight or flight." The "fight or flight" response allows us to move quickly out of the path of a speeding car or protect a child who is in danger.

This response helps us cope with emergencies but harms us when we live each day in a constant state of alertness brought about by a series of stressful situations. A little stress provides motivation, but a hectic, stress-filled life can lead to unhealthy ways of escape.

Tobacco use is a way of both physical and psychological escape from stress. This escape, however, is temporary and deceptive. One cigarette leads to another. And the tobacco which once offered calmness and enjoyment becomes a trap. If the body does not receive its dose of nicotine, it creates stress symptoms as it demands that the addiction be fed.

**Stress symptoms**

Just as each of us find differing events stressful, we have personal ways that we respond to stress. These responses are called stress symptoms.

 **Below circle phrases which best describe your response to stress. It may help to think of one situation which caused you stress during the past week and how you felt.**

- pounding heart
- chest pain
- tight neck and shoulders
- high blood pressure
- cold or sweaty hands

- eyestrain
- upset stomach
- teeth grinding
- headaches
- constipation

- nervous tics
- fatigue
- rashes
- excessive sweating
- diarrhea

## Ways of Coping with Stress

*Your stressors may not change, so you will have to learn some different ways of managing them.*

In the past, you have coped with stress by using tobacco. You avoided or reduced the stress of difficult situations by using tobacco. Now you have stopped using tobacco, and the results will be worth it! However, your stressors may not change, so you will have to learn some different ways of managing them. You probably already have techniques for managing stress other than smoking or using smokeless tobacco.

✎ **Check any of the following techniques you have used in the past.**

❑ Relaxation techniques such as deep breathing
❑ Problem solving
❑ Time management
❑ Spiritual rest

The next four lessons will explain each of these stress management techniques. You will learn different ways of managing stress.

## Christ as Our Role Model in Stress Management

Although Jesus Christ was God in human form, He was not exempt from stress. He experienced the same problems you do. Jesus experienced physical problems of hunger, fatigue, and perhaps even sickness. He experienced the psychological stress of coping with the doubt of His followers and the emotional and physical abuse of those who wanted to kill Him. Jesus had interpersonal stress with His mother, family, the disciples, and the religious leaders. At the crucifixion, Christ experienced stress which has never been experienced by any other human. Jesus is our perfect example when it comes to managing stress. Jesus managed stress by:

1. Remaining focused on His goal. Jesus did as His father wished even when it demanded His life. Read Luke 22:41-42.
2. Keeping His priorities straight. Jesus knew how to separate the essential from the unimportant. Read Luke 12:22-34.
3. Putting spiritual health first. Jesus placed spiritual needs before physical or psychological ones. When time was precious, He chose to pray. When the task ahead looked difficult, Jesus prayed. When the needs of those around Him exhausted Him, He prayed. Read Mark 1:35.

Jesus Christ had even more stress than you or I. He coped by relying on the power of His relationship with God the Father.

✎ **In what ways are you being called to a life that is more like that of Jesus? Write your response as a personal prayer to God.**

_____

_____

_____

After you have suffered for a little while, the God of all grace, who called you to His eternal glory in Christ, will Himself perfect, confirm, strengthen and establish you.

—1 Peter 5:10

✎ **Begin to memorize your Scripture verse for this week. Write the verse on a card to carry with you. Whenever you do some repetitive task like get a drink of water, review the verse.**

<table>
<tr>
<td>

**DAY**

**2**

</td>
<td>

# Using Relaxation Techniques

</td>
</tr>
</table>

*Come to Me, all who are weary and heavy-laden, and I will give you rest. Take My yoke upon you, and learn from Me, for I am gentle and humble in heart; and you shall find rest for your souls. For My yoke is easy, and My load is light.*

—Matthew 11:28-30

God taught me the meaning of Matthew 11:28-30 in an unforgettable experience recently. I had a problem. The apex of my crisis found me standing in my kitchen filled with anger and crying out, "God, you lied. You said that your yoke was easy and your load was light; and it's a lie." Before the thought was completed and out of my mind, God spoke to me. He said, "I'm not carrying this load; you are." And immediately I knew it was the truth. I was trying to deal with the problem by myself, and it was too big for me. The relief which followed my surrender to Christ was wonderful.

*I was trying to deal with the problem by myself, and it was too big for me.*

In this lesson you will examine several specific actions you can use to deal with stress without resorting to nicotine. At the end of today's lesson, you will decide which method(s) to use as part of your stress-management program. Whatever methods you choose, remember daily submission to Christ is the heart of stress management.

**Method 1: Meditation**
Meditating on Christ is different from a Bible reading and prayer time. It means focusing on the power and peace of God and allowing His Spirit to fill you. Begin by finding a peaceful, relaxing location which is free of distractions. Sit or lie in any comfortable position. Release all of your concerns and fears to God. Allow God's love and peace to enter your mind. Ask God to come close as you draw away from the distractions and worries of life. You might want to use relaxed breathing or imagery as part of your meditation.

 **When could you practice God-focused meditation?**

_____

**Method 2: Fasting**
In a sense, you are fasting from tobacco. You are going without it as a person might go without food. Have you ever fasted for spiritual or medical reasons? If so, you probably got hungry. If your fast lasted very long, perhaps you got so hungry that all you could think about was food. When you first stopped using tobacco, you experienced a craving for nicotine and other symptoms of withdrawal. You still may be experiencing some of these symptoms or sometimes have an urge to use tobacco. Withdrawal is a sign that you were controlled by tobacco. One of the benefits of fasting is that fasting demonstrates to us what really is going on in our lives. Fasting reveals the things that control us.

 **Do you agree with the statement that fasting reveals what controls us?**
❏ **Yes** ❏ **No**

 **In the margin box describe how this statement relates to your nicotine dependence.**

---

**Fasting from nicotine reveals to me—**

_____

_____

_____

_____

_____

_____

Each time you tried and failed to give up nicotine may have revealed its control. In Bible times, people fasted by going without food They did this for a spiritual purpose. However, you can benefit from fasting from other things. You might fast from the media, television and radio, newspapers and magazines, or even people. Fasting from these things will reveal to you whether or not you are dependent or controlled by them. During your fast, spend extra time in meditation and prayer to deepen your relationship with Jesus.

*Fasting from these things will reveal whether or not they control you.*

✎ **Check each type of fasting that may benefit you.**

❑ Fasting from your usual schedule. Drive to a quiet, outdoor place. Spend an hour or more each day reading the Bible, praying, and walking. Do not speak during this time unless it is necessary.
❑ Fasting from the media. Spend an entire day without reading newspapers or watching television. Use the extra time listening to Christian tapes or talking with other believers.
❑ Fasting from electronic entertainment. Involve your entire family in leaving televisions, radios, electronic games, and computers turned off for one evening. Spend the time together playing games, reading aloud, biking, or talking.

✎ **Describe any other types of fasting that you would like to try.**

_____

_____

**Method 3: Physical Activity**
Physical activity is another way of managing stress. Regular exercise produces both mental and physical benefits because it produces a calming effect that lasts for a period of time after you complete the activity.[1] Some forms of aerobic exercise such as swimming and running can bring about a state similar to that of meditation.

*Regular exercise produces both mental and physical benefits.*

You should always consult your physician before making any major change in physical activities. Even if you are not able to begin an exercise program, you can reduce physical tension by practicing stretching exercises. A physician or a physical therapist can offer suggestions for stretches which will relieve tension in your neck, shoulders, and back. These small stretches can be used during times you formerly took smoke breaks and help reduce mental and physical tension.

✎ **What type of physical activity do you now do regularly?**

_____

✎ **How is it helpful in reducing stress symptoms?**

_____

**Method 4: Relaxed or Deep Breathing**
Deep breathing focuses on breathing with the bottom or lower part of the chest or diaphragm rather than the upper lungs. Take a normal breath. Did your upper chest or shoulders move? If so, you were probably breathing from your upper lungs. Take another breath, but this time try to draw air into the

very bottom of your lungs. If your lower chest or stomach moved, you probably did it right.

When we are tense or stressed, we tend to take short, rapid breaths from the upper chest. Simply focusing your attention on taking slow, deep breaths is relaxing. You probably do this kind of relaxed breathing just before falling asleep at night. Practice using this method of taking slow, deep breaths periodically throughout the day—especially as a way of coping with the urge to smoke or use tobacco.

Relaxed breathing is as easy as 1-2-3.
1. Inhale slowly while counting to four.
2. Hold your breath briefly.
3. Then exhale slowly while counting to four.

Repeat this pattern two or three times, and then resume breathing normally. These slow, deep breaths will relax you physically. They will also relax you mentally by getting your mind off tobacco. This simple technique has benefited many recovering smokers. You can use the technique in any situation.

When I stopped smoking in 1975, I used a breathing technique which helped me a great deal. I mimicked smoking by holding a straw to my mouth and inhaling deeply. Next I would hold my breath for a few seconds and then exhale slowly through pursed lips. I'm not sure why, but this type of breathing had a calming effect on me. I've suggested it to a lot of people who were giving up cigarettes; most have found it useful.

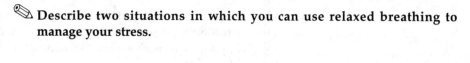 **Describe two situations in which you can use relaxed breathing to manage your stress.**

_____

_____

**Method 5: Imagery**
You can use imagery to help yourself relax. You may combine imagery with meditation or deep breathing, or you may use it by itself.

1. Lie or sit in a quiet place where you will not be interrupted.
2. Close your eyes and concentrate on making all of your muscles as inactive as possible.
3. Consciously relax each muscle until you feel very relaxed and relieved of tension.
4. Think of a place such as your favorite vacation spot. Involve as many of your senses as possible.

If you imagine yourself on a beach, try to hear the sound of waves lapping and feel the warm sun overhead. Try to capture the smell and feel of a cool ocean breeze. Picture wild flowers growing at the edge of the beach. Do not visualize other people in your relaxing scene. Picture yourself alone with God, relaxing in the beauty of His creation. Spend as much time as you wish in your mental vacation spot. When you let go of your imaginary scene, carry the feeling of peace and relaxation with you as you return to your normal activities.

**Special Issue Alert**

*Many false and dangerous teachings and practices involve the use of so called spirit guides and guided imagery. Beware of any book, tape, or teacher who advocates the use of imagery to contact spirits or obtain special or hidden wisdom.*

You may use the same imaginary spot each time you relax or you can vary it. You might visualize peaceful scenes such as a beach, a forest, fields of waving wheat or wild flowers, or a peaceful lake. You might imagine yourself in a field of wildflowers watching clouds drift overhead, or you could be in a boat drifting gently down a peaceful stream.

 **What scene would you find relaxing to visualize?**

_____

**Preventing interruptions**

Planning ahead can prevent unwanted interruptions during your relaxation periods. If you are at home, tell your family that you will be relaxing for about 30 minutes, and ask not to be interrupted unless it is an emergency. If you have young children, arrange for someone else to care for them during your relaxation period. The more you practice any relaxation technique, the better you will get at relaxing. After a few weeks, you will be able simply to close your eyes and relax in any situation. Even a few minutes at work in some quiet spot can do a lot to restore your peace of mind.

### Other Techniques

You may use many other techniques to relax. Books, audio and video cassettes, and other materials on stress management are available in Christian bookstores. No matter what method(s) of relaxing you choose, make it a routine part of your life. Like any other skill, the more you practice relaxing, the better you will get. The greatest benefit comes when you schedule a time to relax each day. You can prevent boredom by varying your activities.

If you have many stressors or are having difficulty coping because of life problems, seek counseling. You may call your minister or schedule an appointment with a Christian counselor. Just talking about your burdens usually helps.

 **In the margin box write a prayer. Thank God for the progress you are making. Seek His wisdom and strength as you continue your recovery.**

➢ **Spend a few minutes practicing your Scripture memory verse. You can meditate on Scripture as a way of dealing with stress.**

**Dear Father—**

_____

_____

_____

_____

_____

_____

**DAY 3**

# Solving Problems

*The rabble who were among them had greedy desires; and also the sons of Israel wept again, and said, "Who will give us meat to eat? We remember the fish we used to eat in Egypt, the cucumbers and the melons and the leeks and the onions and the garlic, but now our appetite is gone. There is nothing at all to look at but this manna.'*

—Numbers 11:4-6

Remembering the past can be a problem. How quickly the Israelites forgot the bad part of living in Egypt! They remembered how tasty the fish were, but they forgot the harsh demands of slavery. They remembered the fruits and vegetables but forgot about making bricks without straw. They remembered having their appetites satisfied and forgot how God had brought them out of slavery, destroyed their enemies, and even prospered them. While making the journey toward the new land, they groaned at their misfortune.

You too are journeying to a new way of life. At times you will miss things about the old life. You may miss the comfort of relaxing with a cigarette after work. You may miss visiting with a friend over coffee and a smoke. You may miss having something to do with your hands or the feel of the tin of tobacco in your pocket. To have these feelings of loss is normal, but do not let your thoughts about them become a longing which draws you back into bondage. When these thoughts come, focus your mind on your reasons for giving up tobacco. Remember the negative parts of your addiction. Pray. Ask God to renew your commitment to abstinence. Keep your face set toward recovery.

## Change Brings New Problems

Living without a substance or action to which we are dependent is not easy. Abstinence creates new problems. Your sleeping and eating patterns may change. You may not know what to do with the extra time you used to spend smoking. Your relationships have changed, and learning to cope with emotions may be difficult, because you are used to covering them up by using tobacco. Now that you are no longer using tobacco, new problems confront you. You have a choice to make. You can either relapse to former nicotine use, or you can find solutions to the new problems.

You can learn many methods for solving problems. The following sequence of steps to solve problems is one method.[2]

**Problem solving**

1. Identify the problem.
2. Write down all possible solutions—even the ridiculous ones.
3. Consider the consequences or outcome of each possible solution.
4. Select the one solution which seems most reasonable.
5. Try out the solution. Use it for enough time to give it a fair chance of working.
6. Evaluate the situation to see if it produced the desired result.
7. If your solution did not produce the desired result, return to the first step and start over.

Kelly is having trouble with abstinence. She is a recovering alcoholic with five years of sobriety. She has been off nicotine for one month and is struggling with the urge to smoke. Mornings are not too bad. She can even cope with breaks with her friends. Evenings, however, are just awful, and she does not know what to do about them. She used to relax with a couple of cigarettes while driving to pick up her children at day-care, and she would continue to smoke throughout the evening whenever she felt tense. Since she quit smoking, Kelly begins to feel stressed when she picks up the children. They are always cranky and hungry, and it seems they begin bickering and crying the very minute she gets them into the car. Things escalate while she gets dinner ready and don't calm down until the children are in bed for the night. When the children finally are in bed, Kelly changes out of her work clothes and collapses into her favorite chair. By then, she is so tense that her deepest longing is just to sit down and have a whole pack of cigarettes. Occasionally, she even ponders having a drink as well. Lately, she wonders if giving up cigarettes was such a good idea.

✎ Use a problem-solving approach to help Kelly. What is her problem?

_____

**Why is she having such difficulty with abstinence?**

_____

**At what time of day does she begin to feel tense? Explain why.**

_____

That Kelly's struggle begins as she picks up her two tired children after work may be obvious to you. Everyone is tired and hungry. More demands exist than Kelly can meet.

✎ **In what ways could Kelly solve her problem? Think of several possible solutions. In the margin list your responses.**

One alternative is for Kelly to carry a nutritious snack in her car for the children and herself to eat during the drive home. This would take the edge off everyone's hunger and provide Kelly with a substitute for cigarettes. Your suggestions may have been different. No one right answer exists. The need is to recognize the problem and find possible solutions.

✎ **Which of the following is Kelly's real problem?**

❑ nicotine withdrawal
❑ a life problem which was aggravated by stopping smoking

Since Kelly has gone an entire month without tobacco, her urge is probably not physical. Her desire for a cigarette likely is a psychological one brought on by her need to find a way to reduce stress. I suspect the second response is Kelly's problem.

Once Kelly identifies the problem and considers possible solutions, she can select a solution to try. The next step in the problem-solving process would be to try the solution for a few days or weeks to see if it solves the problem. At the end of her chosen time period, she would evaluate the situation. If the solution has solved the problem, she can continue with the change. If it has not solved the problem, she can reevaluate the situation and select another solution.

**Evaluating your problems**

✎ **Just as with Kelly, abstinence may be creating some problems for you. Check any of the following problems you are experiencing as a result of giving up tobacco.**

❑ Increased feelings of anger
❑ Feeling awkward in certain situations without using tobacco
❑ Difficulty relaxing after work
❑ Coping with a specific time each day when the urge to use is high
❑ Gaining more weight than intended
❑ Not resting as well as usual
❑ Difficulty getting started in the morning without a cigarette, plug, or pinch
❑ Other: _____

---

**Possible solutions for Kelly—**

_____

_____

_____

_____

_____

_____

## Using the Approach to Solve a Personal Problem

Select one of the problems you identified. Use the problem-solving approach to generate possible solutions. Select one solution and try it next week. At the end of next week, you will be asked to evaluate the effectiveness of your solution.

✎ **What is one problem brought about by abstinence?**

_____

✎ **List all the ways you can think of that you might use to solve this problem. After each solution, give possible consequences. Include both positive and negative consequences.**

_____

_____

_____

_____

✎ **Which solution will you use to change the problem?**

_____

✎ **When will you begin the change?** _____

✎ **When will you evaluate the effectiveness of your change?**

_____

## Not All Problems Can Be Solved

Sometimes we try to solve problems which are not ours to solve. You may want another person to change instead of changing yourself. As you consider problems brought about by abstinence, you need to keep focused on personal problems within your power to change. The "Serenity Prayer" has provided strength and courage to many people. Some problems are outside our control. We must give them to God rather than hold on to them. Note that most people use only the first portion of Reinhold Niebuhr's famous prayer. The complete prayer appears in the margin.

✎ **What is one problem about which you are concerned but over which you have no control?**

_____

✎ **Write a prayer to God about this issue.**

_____

_____

_____

God,
Grant me the serenity
to accept the things
I cannot change, the
courage to change the
things I can, and the
wisdom to know the
difference; living one
day at a time, enjoying
one moment at a time,
accepting hardship as a
pathway to peace;
taking as Jesus did, this
sinful world as it is, not
as I would have it.
Trusting that You will
make all things right if I
surrender to Your will, so
that I may be reason-
ably happy in this life
and supremely happy
with You in the next.
Amen.[3]

# Managing Time Wisely

*Let us also lay aside every encumbrance, and the sin which so easily entangles us, and let us run with endurance the race that is set before us.*

—Hebrews 12:1

As you "raced" through yesterday, how did you use your time? Did you feel as if you were running a rat race against time, and the rats were winning? The chart below contains one twenty-four hour day. Use it to show how you used your time yesterday. Include family, work, personal, and social responsibilities.

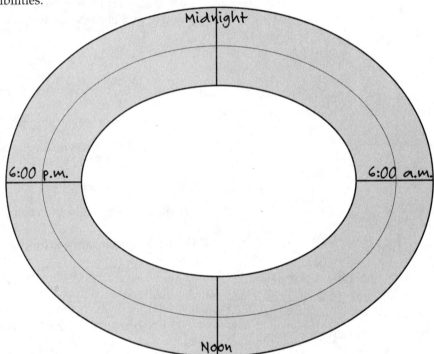

We live in a limited and finite physical world. Only God is unlimited and infinite. The rest of us live between two definite points in time called birth and death. Life is a series of decisions which determine how we will trade the days and moments of our time. We sell our time to such things as our jobs, maintaining our physical bodies, playing with family and friends, and worshipping. When we are young and middle-aged, there never seems to be enough time. And then, due to age, illness, or circumstance, we may have idle time and loneliness.

 **Which kind of time management problem do you have?**

❑ Not enough time to get everything done
❑ Too much time and not enough to do

Time management is important during recovery. You will feel more in control of each day and less stressed if your personal goals are clearly in mind and you are working toward them. Everyone needs goals. If you are too busy, you need to eliminate the nonessentials. If you have too much time, you need to determine productive ways to fill your time.

✎ **Complete the following chart to evaluate your time management skills.**

|  | Never | Sometimes | Often | Always |
|---|---|---|---|---|
| Have difficulty saying no | ❏ | ❏ | ❏ | ❏ |
| Feel disorganized and out of control | ❏ | ❏ | ❏ | ❏ |
| Think every task must be done perfectly | ❏ | ❏ | ❏ | ❏ |
| Having difficulty sleeping | ❏ | ❏ | ❏ | ❏ |
| Just let things happen rather than set goals | ❏ | ❏ | ❏ | ❏ |
| Late for appointments | ❏ | ❏ | ❏ | ❏ |
| Spend time hunting for lost or missing items | ❏ | ❏ | ❏ | ❏ |
| Feel as if others take advantage of you | ❏ | ❏ | ❏ | ❏ |
| Irritated by interruptions | ❏ | ❏ | ❏ | ❏ |
| Think you have too much to do | ❏ | ❏ | ❏ | ❏ |
| Feel impatient with others | ❏ | ❏ | ❏ | ❏ |
| Feel guilty when relaxing or doing nothing | ❏ | ❏ | ❏ | ❏ |

All the items on the above chart can be symptoms of poor time management. Look at the items for which you checked *Always*. If you have several of these symptoms, you need to consider changes in the way you deal with time.

The following guidelines can reduce time management stress.
1. **Simplify.** If someone else can do it, let them. If you don't really need it, give it away.
2. **Prioritize.** Set realistic and achievable long-term and short-term goals. Decide what you want to accomplish during this year, this week, and this day.
3. **Control your schedule.** Remember, however, that people are more important than programs or projects. Make time for the people and things you enjoy.
4. **Organize.** Keep things in their place. It's a lot easier to put things away after you use them than it is to hunt them later.
5. **Recognize that not everything is worth doing well.** Learn to tolerate some confusion and disarray; the world won't end if the bed is left unmade.

> *In your journal today, write about any things you no longer do which once brought you joy. It might be playing the piano, reading for fun, or singing in the shower. Determine to put these things back into your schedule.*

**Too much time**

Too much idle time can be a bigger problem than the stress of too much to do. Everyone needs to feel needed and productive. Everyone needs goals and a purpose in life. God does not give life to any person accidentally. He has a purpose for each day given you. You need to find that purpose. Consider volunteer work at your church, local school, hospital, or care home. Get a calendar, and make specific plans for each day. Enroll in a continuing education course, or join a reading group. Many people in your community need your help. Time is a gift from God; use it wisely.

➤ **Take time to pray about your time and schedule and the stress of too much or too little time.**

*God, I humbly thank You for the time You have given me. I have such comfort in knowing that Your care for me began when I was still unborn and that You have set the boundaries of my life. Please make me wise—wise enough to live each day in the glory of Your love and the peace of Your presence. Keep me centered on You and Your will in each decision I make. Allow me the spiritual strength of Your rest in my relationships and responsibilities. Help me make today count. I love You, Lord. Amen.*

# DAY 5

# Taking a "Sabbath" Rest

*By the seventh day God completed the work which He had done, and He rested on the seventh day from all His work which He had done.*
—Genesis 2:2

Why did God rest on the seventh day? Was He tired from the work of creation? The answer, of course, is no. God established the seventh day, called the Sabbath in Old Testament times, as a day of rest for us. One reason He set it aside was to remind us of our need for rest. The primary reason God set aside the Sabbath was so that we could worship Him. God gave us six days in which to work, but He blessed the seventh day as one of worship.

You have thought a lot this week about the stress in your life. You can use the techniques discussed to reduce tension and anxiety and bring order into your days. But the one thing you must not overlook is the need for spiritual rest. Christ is our role model. The Bible tells us that Jesus frequently went away alone to pray. He also went to the temple on the Sabbath to worship. If Christ, who was God's Son, needed spiritual rest, we certainly need to do the same.

As you plan for the coming weekend, give three things priority.
1. Spend time with your family and/or friends.
2. Spend time outside and enjoy God's world.
3. Attend a worship service in the church of your choice.

✎ **How many days have you been tobacco-free since you began your recovery?** _____

✎ **Use the following activity to evaluate your progress and think about changes you have made. Mark an item *yes* if you did that activity and *no* if you did not.**

## WEEKLY PROGRESS CHECK

| ACTIVITY | YES | NO |
|---|---|---|
| **Physical** | | |
| • Increased physical activity level | ❑ | ❑ |
| • Managed withdrawal symptoms without tobacco | ❑ | ❑ |
| • Felt rested most days | ❑ | ❑ |
| • Drank less caffeinated beverages | ❑ | ❑ |
| • Used oral substitutes (sugarless gum, cinnamon sticks, toothpicks, sugarless hard candy, fresh vegetables, or other) | ❑ | ❑ |
| **Psychological** | | |
| • Motivated to remain smoke-free | ❑ | ❑ |
| • Practiced deep breathing | ❑ | ❑ |
| • Avoided stressful situations as much as possible | ❑ | ❑ |
| • Rewarded myself at least once this week for not smoking | ❑ | ❑ |
| • Changed routines at high risk times of day or situations (morning when waking, after meals, driving, with coffee or cola) | ❑ | ❑ |

**Interpersonal**

|  | YES | NO |
|---|---|---|
| • Attended support group or a 12-Step group | ❑ | ❑ |
| • Avoided others smoking whenever possible | ❑ | ❑ |
| • Shared my progress with one person | ❑ | ❑ |
| • Practiced open communication about my feelings | ❑ | ❑ |
| • Observed nonsmokers to see what they do in certain situations | ❑ | ❑ |

**Spiritual**

|  | YES | NO |
|---|---|---|
| • Read Bible regularly | ❑ | ❑ |
| • Prayed regularly | ❑ | ❑ |
| • Completed workbook assignments for the week | ❑ | ❑ |
| • Attended at least one worship service or Bible study | ❑ | ❑ |
| • Continued to turn my addiction over to Christ | ❑ | ❑ |

The goal is to make change in each of the four dimensions of life: physical, psychological, interpersonal, and spiritual health. Next week try to do at least one thing in each area, but do not be discouraged if you are not making changes in all four areas. It takes many weeks to achieve the kind of balance necessary to healthy recovery.

 **Were you able to follow your weekly plan for this week? Evaluate the effectiveness of this week's plan and develop a new plan for the upcoming week. Use some of the suggestions from unit 4 that you have found helpful.**

## Preparing for the Support Group Session

As you get ready for this week's support group session, be prepared to share the following. Remember to pray daily for each member of your group.

1. Stress management techniques you tried this week with good results.
2. Any problems or concerns you have about abstinence.
3. Personal goals for next week.
4. Personal addictions other than tobacco, either past or present.

---

[1]D.E. Larson, *Mayo Clinic Family Healthbook*, William Morrow and Company, Inc., New York, 1990, 405.

[2]F.L. McClain & R.D. Hurt, "Extinguishing the Smoking Lamp," *Professional Counselor*, Feb. 1994.

[3]Reinhold Niebuhr, "The Serenity Prayer," (St. Meinrad, IN: Abbey Press).

# Caring for God's Temple: Diet and Exercise

**Growth Goal:**
This week you will continue to work on recovery by considering changes in your diet and physical activity.

---

## ONE TRY LEFT IN ME

Max's Story: The last time I quit smoking was three years ago. It has taken me this long to work up enough courage to try again. Right now, I think I have one more try in me. I've got to succeed this time. I quit twice using hypnosis, and one time I went to a group program at a hospital.

The longest I ever made it without smoking was six months, and that time I gained 40 pounds. I was also actively drinking alcohol at the time. I'm a recovering alcoholic with eight years of sobriety, and this time I know I can't turn to alcohol to help me cope with not smoking. I don't know if I can make it without any sort of chemical to pull me through, and I sure don't want to gain as much weight as I did last time. I get scared just thinking about not smoking.

In this unit you will consider ways your diet and exercise can enhance rather than undermine your recovery.

---

**What you'll learn**

This week you will—
• evaluate your health in diet and exercise and decide if you need to make changes in these areas;
• review your risk of turning to other addictions during recovery;
• understand healthy eating habits;
• describe the benefit of exercise during recovery and make plans for personal changes;
• understand the importance of consistent discipline in diet and exercise to prevent relapse.

**What you'll study**

| Setting a Goal for Good Health | Food and Other Addictions | Healthy Eating Habits | Health Through Exercise | Building Endurance |
|---|---|---|---|---|
| DAY 1 | DAY 2 | DAY 3 | DAY 4 | DAY 5 |

**This week's passage of Scripture to memorize—**

**Memory verse**

*But man lives by everything that proceeds out of the mouth of the Lord.*
—Deuteronomy 8:3

<table>
<tr><td>

**DAY**

**1**

</td><td>

# Setting a Goal for Good Health

</td></tr>
</table>

Turn to the course map in the back of this book. Study it for a few minutes and consider where you are in the process of recovery. In the first two weeks you prepared for abstinence by:
1. Admitting your addiction to nicotine.
2. Looking to God as the source of power for the abundant life.
3. Surrendering your life and addiction to God for forgiveness and healing.

Next, you began the race of recovery and spent two weeks in the early action stage. You began the process by managing withdrawal and beginning life changes which support your abstinence. Look back at the Wall of Addiction which you are leaving behind. The addiction was powerful. Don't expect it to let you go without a fight. From time to time, you will feel its pull. You will struggle in certain areas more than others. That is normal.

As you continue progressing on the track of recovery, don't worry about conquering each step. Try to make small changes for which you feel ready. No one can or should try to do everything discussed in this book. You are responsible for selecting those changes in either attitude or action which are right for you. If you know you should make a particular change but do not feel ready, surrender that concern to God in prayer. Making small changes each day will eventually bring you to your goal. You cannot "get it right" the first time; you do not need to. You are not perfect. God does not expect you to be. His love is not conditional on whether you do recovery "right." God wants you to relax and let His Spirit lead. Focus on God's blessings in your daily life. Learn to ask for His strength and joy in the small things. Practice living one day at a time in God's peace and joy.

## The Importance of Diet and Exercise

This week, you will continue the action stage of recovery by considering the role of diet and exercise. Because weight gain is one of the main reasons people give for relapsing, you will be wise to avoid or minimize weight gain. Diet and exercise can improve your health. The reasons for including diet and exercise in your recovery program include:
1. They are positive actions which will improve your health.
2. Diet and exercise encourage recovery and help prevent relapse.
3. Both create positive changes in self-confidence and well-being.

But Daniel said to the overseer whom the commander of the officials had appointed ... "Please test your servants for ten days, and let us be given some vegetables to eat and water to drink. Then let our appearance be observed in your presence, and the appearance of the youths who are eating the king's choice food; and deal with your servants according to what you see." So he listened to them in this matter and tested them for ten days.

—Daniel 1:11a,12-14

Daniel and his three friends were offered the best food and wine of the king's table, but they refused it and asked for vegetables and water instead. (See the Scripture in the margin.) Daniel had a concept of health which included eating certain kinds of foods and abstaining from others. Even in those days, certain tempting foods were harmful to the body. Daniel knew that even though the king's food was thought to be the finest, it was not best for him. The reluctant guard agreed to a 10-day test. At the end of the test period, Daniel and his friends were healthier than the young men who had eaten the king's food and drunk the king's wine. Although Daniel was a prisoner of war, he was in an unusual situation. The king had given orders that he receive the very finest food and drink available, but even in the midst of a difficult situation, Daniel stuck to his personal faith and lifestyle.

Like Daniel, you are in the midst of a challenging situation. You may think this is a bad time to focus on making changes in your diet and physical activity level, but actually it is a good time. You have already made a commitment to good health by deciding to give up tobacco. You will find that the time and effort necessary to healthy eating will support that commitment.

✎ **How would you describe your general health?**

❑ poor ❑ good ❑ excellent

✎ **Below describe what the phrase *good health* means to you.**

_____

_____

Perhaps you wrote that good health is the ability to be physically active, mentally sound, or free of disease. Good health is more than a matter of having good genes. It is consistently making choices which result in wellness. Good health is a goal which pulls you away from addiction and forward into recovery. You are not just moving away from addiction; you are also moving toward the positive goal of good health.

✎ **Name one or two of the healthiest people you know. Describe their lifestyles. Include information about their diet, exercise, ability to handle stress, spiritual faith, attitudes about life, and relationships with other people.**

_____

_____

_____

_____

This week, talk to one or both of the persons you named. Find out how they organize their schedule to include healthy actions. Ask how they handle stress and about the benefits of their healthy lifestyle. Learn about their food and exercise choices. Ask for their support as you become healthier.

✎ **Have you changed your eating habits since you quit using tobacco?**
❑ Yes ❑ No **In the margin box explain how.**

✎ **Which of the following changes in diet and exercise are you able or willing to make at this time?**

❑ I am unable or not ready to make any changes in the areas of diet and exercise at this time.
❑ I am already healthy in these areas and do not need to make changes.
❑ I need to make changes in my diet and my exercise routine and will consider doing so at a later time.
❑ I am willing to make one or two small changes.
❑ I will make moderate changes in these areas as part of my recovery process.
❑ I will make major changes in one or both of today's areas immediately.

**How I have changed eating habits—**

_____

_____

_____

_____

_____

But man lives by everything that proceeds out of the mouth of the LORD.
—Deuteronomy 8:3

 **Begin to memorize Deuteronomy 8:3b, your Scripture memory verse for this week. Write the verse on a card to carry with you. Practice repeating the verse through the day.**

DAY

2

# Food and Other Addictions

*And He humbled you and let you be hungry, and fed you with manna which you did not know, nor did your fathers know, that He might make you understand that man does not live by bread alone, but man lives by everything that proceeds out of the mouth of the LORD.*
—Deuteronomy 8:3

An earlier lesson described how the children of Israel longed for the foods they had enjoyed during captivity. God had freed them from slavery and was leading them to a land of blessing, but they ran out of food on the journey and asked God for help. God answered their prayer by sending them a food called "manna." Manna was a wafer-like substance which had a sweet taste and could be eaten in a variety of ways. God supplied the Israelites with fresh manna daily—always just enough with none left over. Although this miraculous food alleviated their physical hunger, it was not emotionally satisfying. They wanted the old pleasurable foods they had eaten while they were slaves in Egypt. God could have given them the foods they craved, but He chose not to. God wanted His people to trust Him to meet their needs. He wanted them to put their spiritual needs before their physical ones.

*God wanted His people to trust Him to meet their needs.*

The people thought their problem was physical; they craved certain foods. God saw their problem as spiritual. They needed to rely on Him to meet all their needs and do what was best for them. The process of recovery involves many needs. You have physical, psychological, interpersonal, and spiritual needs.

 **When you think about your dependence on tobacco, which of the following needs did nicotine seem to fill?**

❑ Spiritual—it met my need for meaning and purpose.
❑ Physical—it relieved my craving and dulled my pain.
❑ Psychological—it calmed my nerves and helped me to cope.
❑ Interpersonal—it was a part of my relationships with others.

You may have checked any or all of the above needs. Addiction is different for different people. As time passes, you may find that your primary focus changes from one need to another. Initially, physical abstinence may be most difficult, but later you may have difficulty handling social situations without tobacco. Or you may battle with the psychological aspects such as coping with stress or managing time. Recovery, however, is primarily a spiritual battle. It is the process of maturing in faith and turning to God to meet your needs. Like the Hebrew people, you may sometimes crave the addiction of your past. You may try to fill with unhealthy foods or other negative choices that void abstinence created. God's goal for you is the same as for all people; He wants you to trust Him. God wants to develop in you a strong character based on your relationship with Him.

**A spiritual battle**

## What about Weight Gain?

*Tobacco use is an extreme weight management program.*

Many tobacco users fear they will gain weight if they give up tobacco. This is not a good reason for continuing to use. Continuing to smoke to "avoid gaining weight is like cutting off your hands to avoid hangnails...."[1] Tobacco use is an extreme weight management program. First of all, it may not work. Additionally, you must consider the negative health consequences which may result. The few pounds which you might gain as a result of giving up tobacco do not compare with the enormous costs, pain, and suffering you risk by continuing to use.

While some people do gain weight after giving up tobacco, not everyone does. The *Mayo Clinic Family Health Book* says: "a modest, temporary weight gain is a small price to pay for eliminating what may be your single greatest overall health risk and, specifically, for significantly decreasing your chances of having cancer or heart or lung disease."[2]

Nicotine plays a role in weight management in the following five factors.
1. Smoking at the end of a meal signals you that eating is over. When you stop smoking, no signal tells you to stop eating. So you eat more food than usual.
2. Many ex-tobacco users crave sweet foods during the early stage of recovery. One woman who seldom ate desserts found ice cream difficult to resist during withdrawal.
3. Some people substitute eating for smoking. They put food instead of a cigarette or smokeless tobacco in their mouths. This results in more calories and potential weight gain.
4. Food simply smells and tastes better after you have given up tobacco.
5. Nicotine is an appetite suppressant and reduces the amount of food desired. Probably the primary reason people gain weight during abstinence is because they are no longer experiencing the appetite suppressant action of nicotine. Smokers, in general, weigh slightly less than nonsmokers.

**Food tastes better**

All of these factors may result in more food consumed and in weight gain. Because the physical and psychological effects of nicotine differ from one person to another, it is impossible to determine which of the above issues may be true for you. The best decision is to make abstinence from tobacco your primary goal. If you do gain weight, you can lose it after you are comfortable in your nicotine recovery. However, you can avoid or minimize weight gain by making some modest changes in the foods you eat and by increasing your physical activity level. The following suggestions may be all you need.

1. Limit or avoid dessert-type foods which are high in refined sugar. Eat naturally sweet foods such as fresh or dried fruits. Sugar-free substitutes are available if you wish to use them.
2. Limit or avoid foods high in fat. Use skim milk and low fat cheese, and limit the amount of fried foods you eat.
3. Eat more fresh vegetables. They are a healthier substitute than nuts, chips, snack crackers, or candy, and they satisfy the need to crunch.
4. Select a signal or cue for the end of your meal. This might be a glass of water, a cup of decaffeinated coffee, a piece of chewing gum, or brushing your teeth.
5. Get up and leave the table. Do not linger.

6. Serve on a plate the food you will eat. Avoid serving dishes which offer second helpings.
7. Eat at regular meal times and avoid snacking between meals except for low calorie foods and beverages.

Making any of these changes in your eating habits can help keep your weight under control during the early weeks of abstinence. Pay attention to your eating behavior early on because most of the changes are likely to occur then. If you cope with craving or stress during the withdrawal stage by eating, you might continue this new habit after the withdrawal stage is past.

 **Use suggestions from today's study to complete the column titled "Solution" in the table which follows. Skip any row which is not a problem for you.**

### REASONS FOR WEIGHT GAIN DURING RECOVERY

| Tobacco Use | Problem Caused by Abstinence | Solution |
|---|---|---|
| Smoking signaled the end of the meal; | Absence of stop signal leads to eating more. | |
| Chemical effect of nicotine decreases appetite. | Withdrawal triggers craving and desire for sweets to fill "empty feeling." | |
| Tobacco meets need for oral craving or something to put in your mouth. | You use food as substitute for nicotine. | |
| Tobacco damages senses of taste and smell, so you eat less food. | Senses become healthier; food tastes and smells better, you eat more. | |
| Other: | | |

## Other Dependencies

No one completely understands all the reasons a person becomes addicted to a chemical or to a behavior. However, we do know that once a person becomes dependent, for that person to turn to other addictive agents or behaviors is more likely. Sometimes a person who is abstinent from one chemical may turn to another during recovery. Many people who are recovering from nicotine dependence turn to sugar, caffeine, over-the-counter medications, or even alcohol. The desire to find a substitute (especially if it is an addictive substance) is a very real risk for every person during recovery.

**Avoid alcohol**   To avoid alcohol and mood-altering drugs during your recovery from nicotine is especially important. Alcohol relaxes the person and lowers inhibitions making it difficult to stay in control of situations and choices. If you have a drink, you will be more likely to have a cigarette. Many social situations which involve alcohol also involve tobacco use. This combination of less control and exposure to tobacco may create a strong urge to use which is difficult to resist. You can avoid this by abstaining from alcohol, especially during the early stages of recovery.

Caffeine is probably the most commonly used addictive substance in America. People who drink caffeinated coffee or colas or who eat chocolate on a regular basis experience withdrawal symptoms when their caffeine intake is abruptly discontinued. Symptoms of caffeine withdrawal include headache, drowsiness, lethargy, irritability, nervousness, and vague depression. If you are a heavy user of caffeine, you should take care not to increase your caffeine intake during recovery. If you increase your use of caffeine as a way of coping with the desire for tobacco, you may develop symptoms related to high levels of caffeine. If you decide to eliminate nicotine and caffeine at the same time, you will experience withdrawal from both.

Consider the following alternatives if you wish to maintain or reduce the amount of caffeine you use.

**Don't increase caffeine**

1. Do not consume more than your normal amount of caffeine.
2. Do not use caffeine after a certain time of day, perhaps mid afternoon.
3. Buy coffee which is a mix of both caffeinated and decaffeinated brands, or mix your own.
4. Substitute water for the coffee or cola you now drink.

## Advice for Persons in Recovery from Other Addictions

If you are in recovery from any other chemical addiction, you may fear that giving up tobacco will be more difficult than your other addiction. For example, many recovering alcoholics find it difficult to stop smoking. Many reasons for this exist. You may have experienced withdrawal from alcohol or another addictive chemical in the safety of a medical unit or treatment program. Few have the opportunity to experience nicotine withdrawal in that type of secure environment.

A second issue is that if you continue to use one addictive chemical while discontinuing another, the chemical you continue using becomes more important. You may have used the second chemical to cope with the absence of the first. For example, individuals who are addicted to both alcohol and nicotine may decide to give up alcohol. If they continue to use tobacco, they may smoke as a way of coping with the urge to drink. This reinforces the dependence on tobacco and makes it more difficult to give up at a later time.

If these characteristics describe you, you may need additional support during recovery. If you are active in a 12-Step group, ask for a sponsor who is a former tobacco user. Attending or starting a nicotine cessation group could be an alternative. Finally, you can pursue a more intense form of intervention. Outpatient and/or residential treatment programs for nicotine dependent people are available in some medical centers.

Don't think that recovery from more than one addiction is too difficult to do at the same time. All addictions are lived behind the same wall of denial. All recovery demands faith in God. All changes in attitudes and actions work together to strengthen your abundant Life.

**Dave's story**

"When I enrolled in a smoking cessation support group, I had no idea what to expect. I did know that I was desperate to get free of my addiction to nicotine. I had tried everything! Nothing worked! When I was younger I went through a treatment program for alcoholism. After several bouts with treatment and relapse, I finally achieved sobriety. Although I was an active member of Alcoholics Anonymous and knew all about working the steps, I simply could not use them to get free of tobacco. A friend told me about this support group for smokers, and I thought I didn't have anything to lose by giving it a try, so I registered. The first few days of being off cigarettes are still a blur, but gradually things began to make sense. Knowing the other members in my group were counting on me helped. They were people who could relate to how bad I was hooked and who had the same fears and concerns. It was definitely not easy; but little by little, I am beginning to think I might actually make it. It's been almost three months, and I'm still clean and sober."

➤ **Take time to pray about what you are learning, deciding, and experiencing.**

*Thank You, Lord, for giving me the chance to experience recovery from nicotine dependence. I know there is no addiction that You cannot heal. There is nothing I cannot face with Your help. Thank You, too, for the friends who care enough to support me during recovery. Give me courage to make difficult choices. Amen.*

➤ **Repeat your Scripture memory verse, Deuteronomy 8:3b, several times to help you remember the passage.**

**DAY 3**

# Healthy Eating Habits

*Beloved, I urge you ... to abstain from fleshly lusts that wage war against the soul.*

—1 Peter 2:11

**Clyde's story**

"I grew up in a home where eating was a way of life. My mother cooked three 'square' meals a day, and we were expected to clean our plates. I was an active child, however, and did not develop a weight problem until I became an adult. When I was in my mid 30s, I stopped smoking. It was a time when my stress was increasing, and I was working at a sedentary job which led to very little physical activity. My weight began to increase gradually—a few pounds each year. Then I began experiencing shortness of breath and chest pain.

"I made several visits to my doctor. He could detect no heart problems. Finally my doctor sat me down for a talk. He told me that every person's body reacts differently to stress, and that the shortness of breath was in part related to my weight and the pain in my chest was my body's way of telling me it was stressed and out of shape. His advice was that I lose my "spare tire," begin a regular exercise program, and quit worrying about things outside my control. I took his advice and began doing all three. It was some of the best advice I ever received. Although I still find it difficult at times to find time to watch my diet and exercise, my long-term commitment to good health has never wavered. I have also not relapsed to smoking."

## Advice About Eating Disorders

**At war with yourself**

First Peter 2:11 is a powerful verse. Peter tells us that physical desires can actually wage war against the spirit. He urges us to abstain from any physical desire which has the potential to destroy our spiritual relationship with God. Addiction certainly fits into that description. Have you felt at times that you were at war with yourself over addiction—that the spiritual voice within was calling for you to stop before the addiction destroyed you while the voice of the flesh cried out for the nicotine, alcohol, food, or your other "drug of choice"? If so, there is only one answer—abstinence.

If you have an eating disorder such as anorexia nervosa, bulimia, or compulsive overeating, you need extra help during recovery. If you want to lose weight while stopping smoking, you may also need extra help. Most likely your tobacco use is closely associated with these eating disorders. You may smoke instead of eating or to calm down after purging. You may use tobacco for its effect in suppressing the appetite. You may use tobacco as a way of denying the reality of your eating disorder. There may be other personal ways in which tobacco is linked to your food problem. If any of the above apply to you or if you gained a large amount of weight during a past attempt to stop using tobacco, you must address these concerns as part of your recovery from nicotine. Failure to do so may jeopardize your recovery and cause you to relapse.

Many food programs and groups offer help to people with eating disorders. Two programs are offered by the people who provide the LIFE® Support Group Series.[3] One behavioral program, called *First Place*, is a Christ-centered health program which encourages balance in the same four areas of life discussed in this book. The program uses both individual study and group support to help participants develop a healthy lifestyle.

The second program is called *Conquering Eating Disorders: A Christ-Centered 12-Step Process*. It offers an individual study and personal growth approach combined with support group and is based on the Christ-centered 12 Steps.

If neither of these is available or right for you, contact your physician for a referral to another program. If you are not sure whether you can address nicotine dependence and an eating disorder at the same time, get the advice of a professional who can help you develop a recovery plan and arrange for the support you need.

**Ideas for healthier living**

If you know that your food habits are within a normal range of behavior but want to establish healthier ways of eating, the following ideas may help you.

### 1. Eat Breakfast
Many tobacco users skip breakfast and begin their day with tobacco and caffeine. Eating breakfast is important to recovery and building good health. It reaffirms your commitment to abstinence as you begin each day. Breakfast also provides other benefits. A good breakfast improves work performance, increases energy, and improves mood. It increases your metabolic rate and helps prevent weight gain which could cause you to relapse to tobacco use.

Breakfast doesn't have to be difficult or time-consuming. Many healthy options require minimal preparation. Bagels with low-fat or fat-free cream cheese, bran muffins, cereal with low-fat milk, and fruit or fruit juice are quick and healthy choices.

## 2. Drink Water

When you first stopped using tobacco, I encouraged you to drink water because it flushes nicotine and other toxins from your system. Later, I encouraged you to use water as a substitute to relieve the urge to smoke or use tobacco. Now you are in step three of your rebuilding process, and you still need to drink water. Water suppresses the appetite naturally and helps the body metabolize stored fat.[4] Water also helps relieve constipation which can be a problem during abstinence. The amount of water you need to drink each day is about eight 8-ounce glasses.

*Water suppresses the appetite and helps the body metabolize stored fat.*

## 3. Eat Balanced Meals

A healthy food plan may be obtained from many sources including the American Heart Association and the American Diabetes Association. Your personal diet plan should meet your health, age, and activity requirements. A general plan might include foods that are naturally high in complex carbohydrates and fiber such as fresh fruits, vegetables, and grains. The plan would most likely be low in fat and refined and highly processed foods. If you need specific guidelines for a healthy diet, ask your physician to refer you to a dietitian. The *First Place* program is an excellent source of information about healthy eating. (*First Place* food plans follows the American Diabetic Association's food exchange plan.)

✎ **What do you need most today? Below write a prayer. Tell God about your need.**

_____

_____

_____

➤ **Repeat Deuteronomy 8:3b. Continue to memorize the passage. Consider the healthy diet that God intends for you—including both "bread" and the Word of God.**

# DAY 4

# Health Through Exercise

*Simon answered, "Master, we worked all night long and caught nothing. but at Your bidding I will let down the nets." And when they had done this, they enclosed a great quantity of fish; and their nets began to break.*
—Luke 5:5-6

**Lisa's story**

"I just don't have time to exercise. I'm a single parent with kids at home, and I work full time. The commute to work takes me about 30 minutes each way, and my evenings and weekends are filled with shopping, cleaning, and running kids here and there. I know I should exercise and that I would probably feel better if I did, but when would I find time to do it? There's never enough time to get everything done."

Jesus' command in today's verse was not what Simon Peter wanted to hear at the end of a long tiring day. The last thing Peter wanted to hear was that he should work a little more. Peter chose obedience, however, and the reward was a catch of fish that threatened to break the nets. The blessing came when Peter persevered in obedience rather than giving up.

I suggested exercise as a way to manage withdrawal and stress. Exercise also is one of the most effective ways to ensure long-term abstinence.

## Exercise Brings Many Benefits

Exercise plays a key role in preventing relapse because it improves motivation and well-being and reduces stress symptoms. It also helps prevent unwanted weight gain which can lead to relapse. And the positive physical and psychological effect of exercise lasts long after the actual activity has been completed. Exercise tones muscles and increases energy. It may improve your ability to think more clearly and reduce fatigue, tension, and anxiety. It also appears to decrease blood fat and sugar levels. Exercise also helps prevent osteoporosis and improves sleep. Any increase in physical activity can improve your health and sense of well-being.

*Any increase in physical activity can improve your health.*

If you are unable to be involved in aerobic activity, you can still benefit from doing simple stretches and making small increases in your daily activities. You should consult your physician before beginning an extensive exercise program.

## Jesus Is Our Role Model

If Jesus is our perfect role model, do you suppose He was in good physical health? Scripture tells of at least two occasions when He walked 40 miles in a day. Since the Jewish day extended from sunrise to sunset, this meant He averaged 14 minutes per mile.[5] Jesus was healthy physically, psychologically, interpersonally, and spiritually. Walking kept Him physically fit and gave Him time to think and plan. It provided Jesus the opportunity to talk with His Heavenly Father as well as His disciples. All this He did just by walking from one place to another. In all areas of life, Jesus is our perfect role model.

✎ **Check the response that best reflects your current level of exercise.**

❑ adequate          ❑ inadequate          ❑ what is it?

**How many times per week do you exercise?** _____

**For how long each time?** _____

**What physical activities do you most enjoy? In the margin box, name at least three.**

**Can you walk 40 miles in a day and average 14 minutes per mile?**
❑ Yes ❑ No

**Physical activities I enjoy most—**

_____

_____

_____

Not all of us can meet the physical standard of Jesus, but we can start where we are and improve. We can follow the example of Jesus in walking more than we do. Even little ways add up. Walk during your work breaks. Take the stairs instead of the elevator. Park further away from the shopping mall or your office building.

**Consistent discipline**

Be sure to include physical activity in your weekly plan sheet. Remember it takes at least three weeks to form a new habit. Small consistent activity is important for the beginner. Varying your activities will prevent boredom. Also consider whether the exercise session is a time for you to be alone or if you would enjoy getting a friend or family member to accompany you.

➤ **Review your Scripture memory verse for this week.**

**DAY 5**

# Building Endurance

*Therefore, since we have so great a cloud of witnesses surrounding us, let us also lay aside every encumbrance, and the sin that so easily entangles us, and let us run with endurance the race that is set before us, fixing our eyes on Jesus, the author and perfecter of faith, who for the joy set before Him endured the cross, despising the shame, and has sat down at the right hand of the throne of God. For consider Him who has endured such hostility by sinners, so that you may not grow weary and lose heart.*
—Hebrews 12:1-3

Max had always wanted to be the best long distance runner in his high school. Year after year he worked and trained and continued to set goals which were higher and better than the records he had set the year before. Soon Max had a reputation which marked him as a top athlete and a stiff competitor. He was the best. The standard Max set was the one younger students hoped and trained to beat. After high school he went to college and then on to work as a high school track and football coach. His reputation and ability to encourage his students were characteristics which helped his teams win state championships. Max knew how to make winners out of athletes.

When asked the secret of his success, Max said, "If an athlete wants to be the best, he must learn to play the game even when he is hurting." He must learn to play in spite of pain and not use it as an excuse to sit on the sidelines.

A great cloud of witnesses is watching you run the race of recovery. They include angels, friends, and family who are cheering you on to victory. If you are to run the race well, however, you must do some things. You must throw off the weight of addiction and sin. You must run with perseverance or endurance. You must keep your attention focused on Jesus.

We are to run the race of life with perseverance or endurance. Endurance is the quality which separates those who win races from those who do not. We might think that a distance runner needs grace and style, or intelligence and accuracy. But instead of these qualities, today's Bible verse tells us we are to run with endurance.

**Describe how an athlete builds endurance.**

_____

_____

Athletes develop endurance through practice. They begin by making small positive changes. They set aside time each day for their activity. Over a period of weeks, it becomes easier to run the planned distance. Next they increase distance and speed. They eat a healthy diet, get plenty of rest, and avoid addictive chemicals. Consistent discipline builds endurance. Each time they meet or master an obstacle, they become stronger.

You can build endurance in your recovery. You can begin a more active lifestyle. Choose an activity which you enjoy such as walking, running, or stair climbing. Do your chosen activity three or four times a week on an every-other-day schedule. If you plan to begin any major change in your exercise program, get the approval of your physician.

At first, discipline is difficult. You may think you will never be free of the pull of the addiction. But gradually your new actions will become habits, and you will feel comfortable. Each time you face a problem or resist the temptation to use tobacco, you will become stronger and more able to face the next urge. Recovery is a process which takes time and builds endurance. One day, you will be running the track of recovery with ease and freedom.

## Planning for Support Group

1. Complete the Weekly Plan Sheet by filling in the actions you will make next week as part of your recovery plan. Be careful to include adequate weekend planning.
2. Pray for each member of your support group.

---

[1]"Smoking: The Road to a Smoke-free Life," Great Performance, Inc., Chicago. 1987, 15.

[2]_Mayo Clinic Family Health Book,_ William Morrow and Company, Inc. New York, 1990: 414-415.

[3]_First Place_ and _Conquering Eating Disorders: A Christ-Centered 12-Step Process_ may be found at your local Baptist Book Store or Lifeway Christian Store or you may order them by calling 1-800-458-2772.

[4]Carol Lewis and Kay Smith, _First Place: a Christ-Centered Health Program, Members Book_ (Houston: Houston's First Baptist Church, 1992; published by LifeWay Press, Nashville), 79.

[5]C. Lewis, _First Place Orientation Video,_ (Houston: Houston's First Baptist Church, 1992; published by LifeWay Press, Nashville).

# Building Christ-Honoring Relationships

**Growth Goal:**
You will consider changes in relationships with God, family, friends, and co-workers.

---

### I GOT HELP

"I wish I could tell Sarah how tired I am of trying to read her mind and tiptoeing around her violent temper. She just explodes over every little thing. It's impossible to please her no matter how hard I try. Whenever I try to talk to her about problems in our relationship, she just lights one of her infernal cigarettes. Then I know the subject is closed. We both grew up in homes with parents who were active drinkers, and there were lots of arguments. When we married, we agreed that we would never fight in front of our kids the way our parents did with us. We've kept to that agreement, but anymore it seems we don't talk at all.

"The other day, I came home early. Sarah didn't hear me come in. She was talking to a friend on the phone and apparently didn't have trouble telling her friend everything I was doing wrong. It really made me angry. Why does she find it so easy to tell her friend all my failings but won't talk to me about them?"

---

**What you'll learn**

**This week you will—**
- identify three ways you use tobacco: to be alone, to be with others, and to express negative feelings;
- identify the roots of poor relationships and the desire to use external chemicals or actions as a way to escape emotional pain;
- write the characteristics of God as you understand Him and affirm His great love for you;
- practice methods of expressing personal needs clearly and honestly;
- identify your personal support system and take actions designed to strengthen that system.

**What you'll study**

| Interpersonal Relationships | Relationship Problems | Your Relationship with God | Healthy Communication | A Support System for Recovery |
|---|---|---|---|---|
| DAY 1 | DAY 2 | DAY 3 | DAY 4 | DAY 5 |

**This week's passage of Scripture to memorize—**

**Memory verse**

*Your ears will hear a word behind you, "This is the way, walk in it," whenever you turn to the right or to the left.*

—Isaiah 30:21

# Interpersonal Relationships

*Let the words of my mouth and the meditation of my heart be acceptable in Thy sight, O LORD, my rock and my Redeemer.*

—Psalm 19:14

**An individual activity**

Smoking or using tobacco is a way to be alone or separate from other people. Perhaps you can remember using tobacco as a way of isolating yourself from a person or group. Maybe it provided the excuse you needed to relax and be alone. When you were upset, down, depressed, or had an argument with your spouse, you went off to the garage to be alone—with your tobacco. When a relationship was tense, you may have gone on an errand to get away temporarily; and the cigarette you lit as soon as you got in the car was part of the experience. Tobacco use was an easy way of escaping intense feelings or situations. You used tobacco rather than facing and expressing emotions.

✎ **In what ways did/do you use tobacco as a way to be alone and separate from other people?**

_____

_____

✎ **List some feelings with which you have used tobacco to cope or avoid.**

_____

_____

**A social activity**

Tobacco use is an individual behavior, but it is also a social activity. It involves other people. Most people begin using tobacco for social reasons. Tobacco use allows you to belong to a group. It helps you identify with others and creates a sense of belonging. The shared activity bonds you to other people and helps you feel secure and accepted. Initially, tobacco users try nicotine because their friends or a parent use or because they want to be identified as mature. Tobacco use may be a tradition in the family or a social group.

✎ **What social, family, or peer influences played a role in your initial use of tobacco?**

_____

_____

**Three-party relationships**

Social issues were part of why you began using tobacco. You may have started to be accepted with an "in" crowd. You may have certain co-workers with whom you take breaks because they also use. Your spouse and close friends may use tobacco. Nothing is wrong with these relationships; people who use tobacco are not bad. However, your relationships with other tobacco users are really three-party relationships which include you, the other person, and tobacco rituals. Smoking or using tobacco is an activity which you do when you are with these other persons. Use is part of the shared experience. In fact, you may have excluded non-users from your closest relationships.

✏️ **Describe how your tobacco use is part of your relationships with other people. Try to think of specific people such as your spouse, or a friend.**

_____

_____

✏️ **Are you more comfortable with other people if they also use tobacco?**
❑ Yes ❑ No **Explain your answer.**

_____

_____

For many years in America, tobacco use was socially acceptable. A dramatic change has occurred during the past few years, and tobacco use is less socially acceptable. This is primarily due to known health risks associated with its use. Some people find themselves in an amazing situation. Social factors influenced them to begin using tobacco; now these same social factors are among their reasons to quit.

You may feel this change as the number of public places where tobacco is permitted decrease. You may feel resistant to these changes and angered that your "rights" are being violated. You may feel pressured or criticized by family members or co-workers who remind you of the health risks of using tobacco. If this is true of you, make an honest attempt to turn loose of your "rights." Resistance to these changes can only increase your denial and hinder recovery. Accepting the reality of the changes can assist your abstinence.

**An antipersonal activity**

Using tobacco can also be a way of expressing negative feelings about another person or situation. It can be a declaration of your "right" to use and that "nobody is going to stop me." You may even continue to use because some other person wants you to quit. Your resentment of their interference and pushing may lead you to continued use out of spite.

One woman shared that she had quit smoking for several months. Her husband was thrilled because he had wanted her to quit for a long time. One day they got in an argument. She was upset and angry. She drove to a local convenience store and purchased a pack of cigarettes. The one cigarette she smoked was all it took to pull her back into her old addiction. As we talked, she said, "I really showed him; didn't I!"

Walter shared the pleasure of smoking with his wife. When she quit, she began expressing her desire for him also to give up tobacco. When he refused, she asked him to smoke outside rather than inside their home. His feelings in response were strong. Not only had he lost part of the intimacy he and his wife had shared, he felt as if he were also losing his own home. He felt as if his rights were being taken away. He told his wife, "It's my house too, and I am going to smoke in it anytime I want."

_One of the characteristics of addiction is choosing the addiction over personal relationships._

Both of the above stories show how tobacco use can separate you from other people. Sometimes tobacco users feel they must choose either a person or their tobacco. One of the characteristics of addiction is choosing the addiction over personal relationships. This was the case with Walter who chose his right to use tobacco over the feelings of his wife.

✎ Have you ever chosen your tobacco use over a person? ❏ Yes ❏ No Explain.

_____

_____

✎ In your group session this week, be ready to discuss what actions Walter's wife could have taken to encourage him to consider abstinence without making him defensive. Below write your possible suggestions.

_____

_____

_____

*Addicts commonly use tobacco as a way to avoid expressing feelings.*

Tobacco addicts commonly smoke or use tobacco as a way to avoid expressing their feelings—especially in situations involving conflict. You could avoid saying how you felt about a problem by lighting a cigarette. The negative thoughts and feelings could be bottled up inside rather than identified and expressed. Each time you avoided or denied your feelings by using tobacco, you reinforced your dependence. You also hindered the closeness you might have developed with another person if you had risked sharing your feelings.

✎ In what ways was/is your tobacco used as an anti-personal activity which separated you from other people?

_____

_____

Whenever Al became angry or upset, he went out on the porch for a smoke. He discovered that with tobacco he could avoid dealing with painful emotions and even drive away unwanted relationships.

In summary, tobacco use is an:
1. individual activity
2. interpersonal or social activity
3. antipersonal or avoidance activity

Now that you are not using tobacco, you may be aware that your relationships have changed. If your tobacco use was a way to be alone, you need to find other ways of getting a quiet time alone. If tobacco use was a way of being with another person, you can discover other ways of staying emotionally close to this person. If tobacco use was a way of expressing your feelings, you need to expand your ability to communicate clearly and honestly.

✎ Take time to pray. Ask God to help you with your specific recovery-relationship challenges.

✎ This week's Scripture memory verse appears in the margin. Write the verse on a card to carry with you. Review the verse several times as you go through your day.

Your ears will hear a word behind you, "This is the way, walk in it," whenever you turn to the right or to the left.
—Isaiah 30:21

# Relationship Problems

"My name is Rick. When I was a young boy, I swore I would never use tobacco. We were really poor, yet both of my parents smoked. At times I hated their smoking. I can remember being hungry because there was little food in our house, but my parents never seemed to be without cigarettes. It was difficult to understand why there was money for tobacco but not for something to eat. Smoking was repulsive to me; it represented all I did not get from my parents when I was growing up. But in spite of my promise to myself, here I am—a smoker. My parents are both dead, so I can't tell them how angry I feel. I've wasted enough time and money, and I am tired of feeling angry for not keeping my promise to myself."

✎ **As you read Rick's story, what feelings did you experience?**

_____

_____

You may think this kind of experience could only happen in a home where a parent was alcoholic or drug addict. But it is a true story. In Rick's opinion, his parents cared more about their tobacco than they did about whether he and his siblings had enough food to eat. Rick did not feel nurtured, loved, and valued as a child.

**A healthy family**

The ability to develop close relationships is primarily formed by our relationship with our parents or early caregivers. As an infant and a young child, you began to form an opinion of your value which was based on how others treated you. If your parents encouraged and valued you, you probably feel important and capable. However if your early caregivers failed to nurture and value you as a person, you may have a poor opinion of yourself.

✎ **The following list contains characteristics of a healthy family. Mark each item as true (T) or false (F) as it relates to your parents and home when you were a child.**

____ 1. Children felt loved, valued, and protected.
____ 2. Parents encouraged the children to try without the threat of condemnation if they fail.
____ 3. Parents took time to listen to children.
____ 4. Parents corrected the children with caring, consistent, and loving discipline—not with harsh or angry discipline.
____ 5. Family members felt comfortable displaying their affection through touch.
____ 6. The family treated children with respect.
____ 7. Members showed love for one another by talking and listening, and by being supportive of one another.
____ 8. Family members felt free to tell one another how they felt without fear of rejection or betrayal.
____ 9. Members felt safe to discuss any topic: anger as well as joy or fear as well as achievements.
____ 10. Members could tell one another the truth and speak freely about how they felt.

✎ **Total your results. How many items did you mark as true? ____
How many as false? ____**

**Family of origin**

If you marked most of the items in the activity as true, your family was probably a healthy system which nurtured and valued you. You probably have good self-esteem and often feel close to others. Note that some people maintain a "rosy" illusion of their family of origin to avoid facing reality. If you marked several of the items in the activity as false, your family was probably dysfunctional. You may have difficulty sharing your deepest feelings.

✎ **Was your family of origin primarily healthy and nurturing or primarily dysfunctional?**

❑ primarily healthy and nurturing
❑ dysfunctional more of the time than nurturing
❑ almost always dysfunctional
❑ I don't know

✎ **What connections, if any, can you see between your early caregivers and your nicotine dependence?**

_____

_____

**Learn to identify feelings**

Even if you were reared in a nurturing family, you may have some unhealthy ways of dealing with your feelings. If you have relied on tobacco to alleviate or avoid feelings, you may be finding abstinence difficult. Learning to identify and communicate emotions in healthier ways make living without addiction easier. June responded that she learned in her dysfunctional family not to feel or express her emotions. Tobacco helped her to hide her emotions.

➤ **Review this lesson. Take time to pray. Tell God about any self-understanding you are gaining. Ask Him to help you build more healthy and Christ-honoring relationships.**

➤ **Practice your Scripture memory verse for this lesson and review the five other Scriptures you have been learning during this course.**

# DAY 3

# Your Relationship with God

*Now when John in prison heard of the works of Christ, he sent word by his disciples, and said to Him, "Are You the Expected One, or shall we look for someone else?"*

—Matthew 11:2-3

**Marjorie's story**

"Since I was a young child I have thought of God as a kind of angry judge who sat up in heaven waiting for me to make a mistake. When anything went wrong in my life, I blamed God. When I got a divorce, it was God's fault for not fixing things. When I had health problems or trouble with the kids, I blamed God for not making life easier. So many bad things happen in the world around me, and I just could not see God as loving and caring.

*God began to reveal Himself to me through the stories.*

"Then I got sick and was flat on my back for several weeks. I was bored and started reading my Bible—just to see if God had any advice for me. Soon I was hooked and began reading it every day. God began to reveal Himself to me through the stories. I learned that He is a God of great patience and trust. He has given me so much, but all I could see was what I did not have. I don't know why it took me so long to understand that God really loves me. Little by little, I am learning to look at life differently. I try to see God at work around me, and I am trying to trust Him more with my problems.

## Understanding Your Concept of God

At times we all have a difficult time understanding God. Even those closest to Jesus, failed to understand His actions fully. We would think John the Baptist, who is called the forerunner of the Messiah, would have clearly understood that Jesus was the Messiah. But even John had his moment of doubt. In fact, he sent a messenger to Jesus with a question. John was in prison, and he knew he might soon be put to death. Before he died there was one important question he needed answered. He sent a messenger to Christ asking, "Are you the Messiah or not?"

*Now when John in prison heard of the works of Christ, he sent word by his disciples, and said to Him, "Are You the Expected One, or shall we look for someone else?"*

*—Matthew 11:2-3*

This was an unusual question for John to ask. Just a short time earlier, he publicly proclaimed that Jesus was the Messiah. He baptized Jesus and witnessed the dove of the Spirit and heard the voice of God saying, "Thou art My beloved Son, in Thee I am well-pleased" (Mark 1:11). Yet now, John was about to die and was wondering if Jesus really was the Messiah.

Do you ever wonder who God is? Do you ever doubt His activity in your life? Do you have difficulty expressing your real feelings to God? Try to set aside what you have been taught about God and focus on your feelings about God. Your ability to share your deepest feelings and thoughts with God is based on your relationship with Him.

✎ **Read the following Scriptures. In the margin beside each, write the words or phrases which describe God.**

*For I am convinced that neither death, nor life, nor angels, nor principalities, nor things present, nor things to come, nor powers, nor height, nor depth, nor any other created thing, shall be able to separate us from the love of God, which is in Christ Jesus our Lord.*

*—Romans 8:38-39*

*Trust in the Lord forever, For in God the Lord, we have an everlasting Rock.*

*—Isaiah 26:4*

*But God, being rich in mercy, because of His great love with which He loved us… raised us up with Him, and seated us with Him in the heavenly places, in Christ Jesus, in order that in the ages to come He might show the surpassing riches of His grace in kindness toward us in Christ Jesus.*

*—Ephesians 2:4, 6-7*

*See how great a love the Father has bestowed upon us, that we should be called children of God; and such we are. For this reason the world does not know us, because it did not know Him.*

*—1 John 3:1*

As you wrote the characteristics of God, did you fully believe each to be true? They are! You can absolutely know that God loves you. He gave everything He had for you when His Son, Jesus Christ, died on the cross to forgive your sins. God's love is complete; it lacks nothing. God's love is all encompassing; nothing you can ever do can separate you from it. God's love is trustworthy; He will never betray you. God works only for good in the lives of His children. You can depend on God. If others fail you, God never will. Others may attack and attempt to destroy you; God never does. Although others do not understand you, God always does. Your relationship with God is the one constant in all of life. He is the Messiah who loves you and who can free you from addiction and sin!

## How to Communicate with God

"Go and report to John what you hear and see: the blind receive sight and the lame walk, the lepers are cleansed and the deaf hear, and the dead are raised up, and the poor have the gospel preached to them. And blessed is he who keeps from stumbling over Me."
—Matthew 11:4-6

Jesus did not condemn John for doubting who he was. He answered John's question in a way that left no doubt in John's mind. Read Jesus' reply to John's question in Matthew 11:4-6, which appears in the margin.

If John could have questions and doubts about what God was doing in his life, you can too. God is big enough to deal with your questions and doubts. He knows your needs. God wants to meet them through His strength and peace. But He will not give us His gifts unless we ask. As long as we are content to grapple and struggle with life, Jesus will let us. When we recognize our powerlessness and need, He is able and willing to meet our needs.

We need to remember Christ's message to John, "the blind receive sight, and the lame walk." God is in the healing business. He heals physical, psychological, interpersonal, and spiritual illnesses.

✎ **What do you need from God today? Tell Him. Be honest about your feelings and thoughts. Lay aside your old wrong beliefs about God. Ask God for spiritual eyes to see Him as He really is.**

# Healthy Communication

✎ **Review the story of Sarah that began this unit on page 79. Why do you suppose it may be easier for Sarah to talk to her friend than to her husband?**

❑ Less risk—she does not have as much invested in the relationship with her friend.
❑ Greater trust—possibly she trusts her friend but does not trust her husband.
❑ Fear of conflict—Sarah may lack the skills to deal with and resolve conflict.
❑ Low self-esteem—she may be unable to stand up for herself and make her needs known.
❑ Fear of abandonment—she may fear that if she trusts her husband, she will become vulnerable or he will abandon her.
❑ Other _____

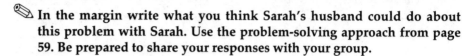

**How does Sarah use smoking to avoid talking with her husband?**

_____

**In the margin write what you think Sarah's husband could do about this problem with Sarah. Use the problem-solving approach from page 59. Be prepared to share your responses with your group.**

## What Sarah's husband might do...

_____

_____

_____

_____

_____

Your ears will hear a word behind you, "This is the way, walk in it," whenever you turn to the right or to the left.
—Isaiah 30:21

Some addicts are addicted to a chemical. Some addicts are addicted to a behavior. One reason nicotine addiction is so difficult to overcome is because it is both chemical <u>and</u> behavioral.

We all have difficult relationships, but some are more difficult than others. When you have tried everything and failed, don't give up before you give God a chance. When you do not know which way to turn, God can give you direction. The most important part of living in faith is learning to hear God's voice. The voice of God can come from in front, beside, above, or within us. Occasionally, we hear the voice of God behind us. In our rush to get things done and make things right, we hurry right on past God—leaving Him patiently waiting for us to realize we have left Him behind. When we are alone and feeling desperate, His quiet voice says, "This is the way; walk in it." Learning to hear and trust the quiet voice of God in our relationships is a difficult part of recovery. We must train ourselves to hear the voice of God. Then we can follow God's leading in our difficult relationships.

The ability to feel and to express feelings honestly reduces stress in relationships. But before you can be honest with someone else, you must first be honest with yourself. Most people who are recovering from addiction find they have not always been honest with themselves about feelings. Instead of acknowledging feelings and expressing them openly, we turn to a substance or behavior. When faced with conflict or a stressful situation, smokers turn to cigarettes. Alcoholics turn to a drink. Compulsive overeaters turn to food. Exercisers turn to running or some other compulsive activity. All are efforts to escape, avoid, or deny uncomfortable feelings. When you want to take the easy way, remember the words of Isaiah, "This is the way; walk in it."

### 1. Healthy Communication Begins with Personal Honesty
Learning to accept feelings which you have not acknowledged in the past is one of the biggest challenges in recovery. After years of turning to a substance or activity outside yourself, to seek healthy ways of thinking feels awkward. Have you said to yourself, "I might as well give up and not try. I'll never be able to stop." If you catch yourself thinking negatively, stop. Visualize a huge red stop sign. Then, change the message you are sending yourself into a positive one. Speak to yourself as if the message were from God. How God would speak to you in the situation? Would He tell you how bad you are and that you are a loser? Or would God remind you that He loves you and wants you to keep trying? Allow God's love and grace into the way you think about yourself. Remember that you are valuable to God.

**What are some negative messages you say to yourself? I have given you an example.**

You are so stupid, you'll never get it right!

_____

_____

_____

I will give thanks to Thee, for I am fearfully and wonderfully made;
—Psalm 139:14

✎ **What are some positive thoughts or Bible verses you could use to replace these thoughts? I have given you a reply to the previous example.**

*I am God's special creation. He says I am wonderful. I simply made a mistake—that is normal, human, and OK.*

_____

_____

_____

**2. Healthy Communication Shares Feelings with Others**
Sometimes to be honest with friends, family, and co-workers is difficult; to avoid sharing true feelings seems easier. You may be like Sarah in this unit's case story. You may use tobacco to avoid conflict with your spouse or loved one but then talk to someone else about your feelings.

✎ **In the margin write the names or initials of individuals you have difficulty talking with openly.**

✎ **Why do you find communication with these individuals difficult?**

_____

_____

Often we avoid speaking the truth to others because we fear conflict. Keeping silent gives us an illusion of peace. It is an illusion, however, because it doesn't work. Each time we keep silent to avoid a confrontation, we deny our right to have certain feelings. We may believe that our feelings do not matter or that they do not matter as much as those of someone else, but the more we stuff feelings inside by refusing to accept and communicate them to others, the greater our inner tension becomes. We feel angry with other people who fail to read our minds. Then we feel guilty for being angry. The result is a no-win situation which alienates us from other people and from God.

You cannot live in the abundance of God's love when you are filled with tension and resentment. The pressure inside will build each time you repeat this cycle—like shaking a bottle of cola. Eventually, the top will blow. When the lid comes off, the contents explode in a torrent of hurtful words and actions. The ability to express your feelings honestly prevents this inner pressure from building and exploding.

**Exploding contents**

✎ **Think about a recent experience when you had conflict with another person. Who was involved? Explain what the conflict was about and what you did, if anything, to resolve it.**

_____

_____

**Were you able to communicate your feelings?** ❏ Yes  ❏ No

**Did your sharing have a positive or negative effect?** _____

[There is] a time to be silent and a time to speak.

—Ecclesiastes 3:7

Knowing what to say and when to say it is a difficult skill involved in honest communication. Ecclesiastes, chapter three reminds us that there is a time to speak and a time to keep silent. Much damage can be done when we get the times mixed up. To risk saying words which will hurt another person is sometimes appropriate, but it should always be done with a caring heart. Sharing feelings in an assertive but caring manner is different than taking advantage of a situation by aggressively attacking another person. If withdrawal has given you excuse to speak unkindly to another person, you may need to apologize for your actions or words.

✎ **Write the names of any persons you have been unkind to during your withdrawal stage. How could you make amends to them?**

_____

_____

**More of Fran's story**

### 3. Healthy Communication Asks for What Is Needed
As a newlywed, for me to ask for help from other people was very difficult. I tried to be perfect in every way and expected others to also be perfect. I expected my husband to do what I wanted without my having to ask. Needless to say, he disappointed me frequently. We normally went out to eat over the weekend. We would get in the car, and my husband would ask, "Where would you like to go?" I always responded, "I don't care; anywhere is fine."

The problem was that I was not being honest. Often I did have a particular place I wanted to eat—or some place I absolutely did not want to go. But I did not tell my husband. Since he is a decisive person and I had withheld my opinion, he decided where we went. Sometimes his decision was right; sometimes it was not. When he guessed wrong, I was resentful and did not enjoy myself. Learning to express my opinion and feelings was liberating. It also did a lot to decrease conflict in our relationship. It made me responsible for my own happiness rather than expecting someone else to make me happy.

*You are free to make mistakes as well as to forgive others for theirs.*

When I understood that God loved me—that I did not have to be perfect—I began living in the love of Christ. I became free to share my hurts and needs with others. You can experience these same blessings in your relationships. You can develop relationships based on mutual love and realistic expectations. When you absolutely know that Jesus loves you, you are free to make mistakes as well as to forgive others for theirs. You come to understand that within the body of Christ, we are all imperfect and we need each other.

➤ **Review this lesson. Write a prayer expressing to God whatever thoughts and feelings you have as a result of your study today.**

_____

_____

✎ **Below attempt to write your Scripture memory verse from memory. You may check your work on page 79.**

_____

_____

# A Support System for Recovery

*And when he [Paul] had come to Jerusalem, he was trying to associate with the disciples; and they were all afraid of him, not believing that he was a disciple. But Barnabas took hold of him and brought him to the apostles and described to them how he had seen the Lord on the road, and that He had talked to him, and how at Damascus he had spoken out boldly in the name of Jesus.*

—Acts 9:26-27

**Paul's support person**

Barnabas gave Paul the support he needed at a critical time. Paul had a bad reputation among Christians because he had persecuted them in the past. After Paul met Jesus, he was a changed person with a new attitude. This resulted in a change in his actions and relationships. Although Paul was a different person, it was difficult for those he had once persecuted to believe that Paul now could be different. They were reluctant to trust him. Barnabas introduced Paul personally and told how he had changed since meeting Jesus. Barnabas' support was the beginning of a new ministry for Paul. Barnabas was Paul's support person.

## Identifying Your Personal Support System

Hopefully, you too have family and friends who support your efforts in recovery. You can encourage them to support you by:
1. identifying those people who support your efforts in recovery;
2. identifying those who have hindered your efforts in recovery;
3. deciding what you want or need from each person;
4. planning a way to communicate with each person.

✎ **On the lines below write the names of people who have been supportive or who have hindered your recovery. Consider family members, friends, co-workers, and acquaintances. After you have written names, write what you need from each person and your plan for communicating with each person.**

| Supportive people | What I need and how I will communicate this need |
|---|---|
| _____ | _____ |
| _____ | _____ |
| _____ | _____ |

| Non-supportive people | |
|---|---|
| _____ | _____ |
| _____ | _____ |
| _____ | _____ |

Your communication plan could include talking to each person individually, sending a card, or making a telephone call. In some cases your plan may be to limit your exposure to people who are "toxic" for you. Dealing with the relationships which have hindered your recovery can be tricky, especially if they are family members or close friends. The ideal solution would be to talk with each person about your feelings with the intent of gaining their support. However, honest communication about your feelings could have a negative result. Your honest words, although spoken in love, might offend the person or harm your relationship. Pray before you take any action. You may need to find a different solution if the person is not one with whom you can share honestly and openly or if your words would do more harm than good.

If you decide to approach those who have hurt or hindered you, remember to stay focused on their actions. Do not attack their personal worth. Express your own feelings without blaming. You might consider saying, "My recovery from nicotine addiction is very important to me. I could use your support. Would you be willing to help me by...?" Be prepared for a negative response. You must allow freedom for them to choose their response without feeling pressured. Your group facilitator will give you a copy of a letter you can give to your support people.

✎ **Below write a personal prayer expressing your thoughts and feelings.**

_____

_____

_____

_____

## The Importance of Your Support Group

As you have already learned, being part of a personal support group creates a unique bond because the rules which you agreed to in the group covenant generate a safe environment of trust. As each member shares feelings, problems, and strengths, others are enriched.

If you have not been an active part of your support group, you are missing a blessing. Make the decision to recommit to your support group this week. Risk sharing your struggles. Ask for the prayers and support of other group members.

✎ **Think about your weekly support group. In what ways has this group enriched your life and benefited your recovery? Have you been able to risk in ways which are new to you? If so, have you been able to carry these abilities over into your everyday relationships?**

_____

_____

_____

You will have an opportunity to share your answers to these questions in this week's support group session.

# Grief and Loss: Casting Your Cares Upon Him

**Growth Goal:**
You will identify personal emotions of grief and be asked to commit these losses to God.

---

### AMBUSHED BY GRIEF

Pat shared the following feelings with a friend after she quit smoking: "My husband, Bill, died unexpectedly five years ago in an automobile accident. My loss was tremendous, but I had two young children to care for and little time to grieve. Our finances were a mess. Bill didn't leave much insurance, so I had to go back to work. My parents helped out with the kids before and after school; I couldn't have made it without them.

"Four weeks ago, I quit smoking and gave up tobacco for good. It's been really difficult. In fact, I am grieving more over the loss of my cigarettes than I did over Bill's death. I feel guilty and don't understand how I could feel this way. How could giving up smoking be a greater loss than the death of my husband? Something must be wrong with me for feeling this way, but I don't know what to do. That's why I decided to talk to you. We've been good friends for a long time, and I know you quit smoking too. I thought maybe you wouldn't be shocked by my feelings and could help me."

In this unit you will examine the common experience of grieving over the loss of an addiction.

---

**What you'll learn**

This week you will—
• identify past and present causes of grief in your own life;
• understand personal feelings within the four stage grief process;
• understand the importance of faith in Christ to making suffering bearable;
• understand forgiveness through Christ's power as a beginning to healing past hurts;
• understand that the love of God is available to you.

**What you'll study**

| Identifying Causes of Grief | Understanding the Feelings of Grief | Resolving Suffering | Forgiving Others | Loving the Way God Does |
|---|---|---|---|---|
| DAY 1 | DAY 2 | DAY 3 | DAY 4 | DAY 5 |

This week's passage of Scripture to memorize—

**Memory verse**

*But He was pierced through for our transgressions, He was crushed for our iniquities; The chastening for our well being fell upon Him, and by His scourging we are healed.*

—Isaiah 53:5

92

# Identifying Causes of Grief

*He was pierced through for our transgressions, He was crushed for our iniquities; The chastening for our well-being fell upon Him, And by His scourging we are healed.*

—Isaiah 53:5

You may feel grief because of the loss of tobacco. This feeling of grief arrives as an ugly surprise. It feels as if a floor of ice has been poured into your life. You skate on an ice rink of grief, with no going back. You have two options. You can sit on the sidelines and moan your losses, or you can put on a pair of skates and learn to skate.

**Like learning to skate**

The process of learning to skate can help you understand the role of grief in recovery. As a beginning skater, you probably held on to the retaining wall or the supporting arm of some other person. Each time you went around the rink, you became more confident. Gradually staying on your feet became easier. Then you were able to take a few steps on your own. Eventually, if you persisted, you could move with confidence and grace over the rink.

You have learned to keep your balance in many situations. The icy floor of grief, however, may be hindering your progress. You may grieve over the loss of tobacco and the comfort it offered. Or, with the comfort of tobacco removed, you may realize that you have deeper personal losses and hurts. These deep personal losses might include a poor marital relationship, unhappiness in your job, or perhaps the abuses you experienced as a child. Now that you are not using tobacco, these inner griefs may surface to cause feelings of pain and loss.

Naomi said to her two daughters-in-law, "Go, return each of you to her mother's house. May the Lord deal kindly with you as you have dealt with the dead and me. May the Lord grant that you may find rest, each in the house of her husband." Then she kissed them, and they wept.

—Ruth 1:8-9

The biblical story of Ruth tells how two women coped with grief and loss. Naomi was an older woman; Ruth was her daughter-in-law. Naomi's husband and both of her sons—one of whom was Ruth's husband—died in the foreign land of Moab. As a result these two women were left to exist in poverty and grief. Naomi decided to return to the land of Israel, so she sent her two widowed daughters-in-law home to their own parents.

Naomi had many reasons to grieve. She had experienced a major move from one country to another. Her sons had married outside her religion. She had suffered the deaths of her husband and her two grown sons. Finally, she was left with the responsibility of caring for her two daughters-in-law. This was not an easy task at a time when women were usually cared for by their husbands and sons. She could apply for no jobs outside the home, no social security existed, and no relatives would take her in.

✎ **Perhaps you have had some of the same losses as Naomi. Check all of the following losses which you have experienced.**

❑ death of your spouse
❑ death of a child
❑ loss of a job
❑ feelings of loneliness
❑ loss of a family member due to a move, estrangement, or death

❑ divorce
❑ move to a different location
❑ financial difficulty
❑ other _____

Perhaps like Naomi you looked for a way of coping with your losses. You may have decided to move, get a new job, or make some other change which would allow you to start over. Naomi decided that she would be better off in her home country of Judah. We have no idea how long after the deaths of her sons it was that she made this decision. In the midst of her grief, Naomi determined to start over. Rather than stay in an impossible situation, she chose change.

✎ **In what ways can you compare your present situation to that of Naomi?**

_____

_____

➤ **If you sometimes have difficulty facing change, use this prayer to guide you in asking God's help.**

*Lord God, thank You for the example of Naomi. I know that with You, it is never too late to start over. I still need Your support and guidance in my grief and loss over tobacco. Please give me Your strength and courage in my weakness. Amen*

✎ **Begin to memorize Isaiah 53:5, your Scripture memory verse for this week. Write the verse on a card to carry with you. Practice repeating the verse through the day.**

But He was pierced through for our transgressions, He was crushed for our iniquities; The chastening for our well being fell upon Him, and by His scourging we are healed.
—Isaiah 53:5

**DAY 2**

# Feelings of Grief

Pat shared the following feelings with a friend after she quit smoking: "My husband, Bill, died unexpectedly five years ago in an automobile accident. My loss was tremendous, but I had two young children to care for and little time to grieve. Our finances were a mess. Bill didn't leave much insurance, so I had to go back to work. My parents helped out with the kids before and after school; I couldn't have made it without them.

"Four weeks ago, I quit smoking and gave up tobacco for good. It's been really difficult. In fact, I am grieving more over the loss of my cigarettes than I did over Bill's death. I feel guilty and don't understand how I could feel this way. How could giving up smoking be a greater loss than the death of my husband? Something must be wrong with me for feeling this way, but I don't know what to do. That's why I decided to talk to you. We've been good friends for a long time, and I know you quit smoking too. I thought maybe you wouldn't be shocked by my feelings and could help me."

✎ **Can you understand Pat's feelings?** ❏ Yes ❏ No

✎ **As Pat's friend, what words of encouragement would you give her?**

_____

_____

*Whatever feelings you are experiencing are normal—for you.*

Perhaps you are like Pat in experiencing grief over the loss of tobacco. Smoking or using smokeless tobacco was like an intimate friend or even a part of yourself. If tobacco was important to you, you need to grieve its loss without feeling guilty. Feelings are neither right nor wrong; they just are. Pat's grief over the loss of tobacco was normal—for her. Whatever feelings you are experiencing are normal—for you. You don't need to hide from them, and you don't have to feel guilty for having them.

In yesterday's Bible passage, we looked at Naomi's grief over the deaths of her husband and sons. She decided to leave Moab and return to Judah. Most likely she wanted to be with friends and family who could offer support in her time of grief. Before she moved, she told her two daughters-in-law to return to their families and look for new husbands. One daughter-in-law, Orpah, was sad but agreed to Naomi's suggestion. Ruth, however, refused. Ruth insisted on staying with her mother-in-law.

So they both went until they came to Bethlehem. And it came about when they had come to Bethlehem, that all the city was stirred because of them, and the women said, "Is this Naomi?" And she said to them, "Do not call me Naomi (Pleasant); call me Mara (Bitter), for the Almighty has dealt very bitterly with me. I went out full, but the Lord has brought me back empty. Why do you call me Naomi, since the Lord has witnessed against me and the Almighty has afflicted me?"

—Ruth 1:19-21

When Naomi arrived at her ancestral home of Bethlehem, she was overcome with her grief. Her feelings of grief were so intense that she could no longer live up to her name which meant *Pleasant*. She told her friends to call her *Mara* or *Bitter* instead. Naomi was angry, bitter, and disillusioned with life and with God. Naomi had an outstanding ability; however, she could face her feelings honestly. She was honest with herself, her friends, and with God. The sad thing about Naomi's anger was that it prevented her from seeing God's blessings. In fact, she said, "the Lord has brought me back empty." Her anger kept her from recognizing the tremendous blessing of Ruth's unconditional love.

Anger is a feeling most people experience in times of grief. Elizabeth Kubler-Ross includes anger in her stages of grief. These stages are: denial, anger, bargaining, depression, and acceptance.[1] Any grieving person may experience these feelings. The feelings do not always come in any certain order, nor do they last for a specific period of time. Each person experiences the feelings and stages of grief in an individual way. If you are grieving, it is impossible to know how long you will stay in each stage. You may move out of one feeling stage but return to it at a later time.

 **The following paragraphs describe the five stages of grief. As you read, underline the feelings, thoughts, or actions you can relate to your tobacco use and recovery.**

**Denial**

We often respond with denial to a crisis or change. We cannot absorb the loss, so our defense mechanism denies reality: *This cannot be true. It has not happened. I refuse to believe it.*

Perhaps you can relate to denial at an earlier stage of recovery from nicotine dependence. You may have denied some medical or health condition. You may have thought or said something like: *My shortness of breath has nothing to do with my smoking.* Or you may have denied your addiction by thinking or saying, *I'm not really addicted to nicotine. I can give it up anytime I want; I'm just not ready.* Denial is powerful. It can prevent you from beginning recovery. It can also creep in during recovery with thoughts like, *I've gone without tobacco for several weeks now. Surely I could have just one cigarette (or chew). I am in control now. Just one won't hurt.* If you are experiencing these thoughts, be careful. They are dangerous expressions of denial which can pull you back into your old addiction.

**Anger**

Anger, the second stage in the grief process, can be a major hurdle to recovery. Sometimes we can remain tobacco-free but stay angry because we gave up tobacco. All recovering addicts feel anger, but some people have more anger than others. People who have already given up one addictive substance or behavior sometimes experience deep anger when they decide to give up their "last vice." They may feel that they have already given up everything else, that smoking or using tobacco was their last pleasure.

If you are angry at giving up tobacco or over some past hurt, acknowledge your feelings. Follow the example of Naomi; confess your feelings to yourself, another person or your support group, and God. Try to understand what is feeding your anger. Ask God to heal the causes of your anger.

**Bargaining**

Bargaining is the third stage in the grief recovery process. When you were still using tobacco, you may have bargained rather than giving up tobacco completely. You may have changed to a brand you thought would be less damaging to your health. You may have switched from cigarettes to smokeless tobacco or a pipe. You may have cut down the amount of tobacco used. All of these were attempts to bargain with tobacco and avoid total abstinence. Now that you are tobacco-free, bargaining can still be a problem. If you have decided that you will remain free of tobacco until a certain date or unless some specific thing happens, you are setting yourself up for relapse. You cannot bargain with addiction.

**Depression**

Depression is the fourth stage. Almost everyone who gives up tobacco experiences some depression. It is an initial withdrawal symptom. Usually depression resulting from withdrawal is temporary and mild. It lasts only the first few weeks and can be overcome by increasing physical activity, talking about feelings, or making minor changes in daily routines. In a few weeks it goes away.

Occasionally, a person who stops using tobacco may become severely depressed. If you have a history of depression or chronically feel "blue," you should watch for the following danger signals which may indicate severe depression.
- Prolonged loss of appetite
- Difficulty getting enough sleep or a desire to sleep a great deal of the time
- Loss of interest in usual everyday activities
- Inability to feel pleasure about usually enjoyable persons or events
- Chronic irritability
- Avoiding other persons
- Feeling hopeless and helpless
- Fatigue
- Preoccupation with the lost person or thing

*Consult your physician if you continue to have difficulty with depression*

Consider the above symptoms and consult your physician if: 1. You have been free of nicotine for several weeks and continue to have difficulty with depression; 2. You have been free of nicotine for a brief time but feel your depression might be more extreme than is normal; 3. You have a personal or family history of depression which concerns you.

If you are experiencing depression, seek medical help rather than relapsing to tobacco use. You may need treatment for underlying medical issues. Your physician can work with you to resolve these issues and allow you to remain tobacco-free.

**Acceptance**

Acceptance is the final stage of the grief recovery process. It means you have admitted your powerlessness over nicotine and have turned to God as the source of healing. Although you recognize personal progress and may feel some confidence in your ability to remain tobacco-free, you also realize the risk of relapse. Honestly accepting tobacco's addicting power over you keeps you from thinking you can be an occasional user.

✎ **Circle the stage(s) of grief which best describe(s) your current feelings.**

Denial    Anger    Bargaining    Depression    Acceptance

✎ **Why do you think you are in the stage or stages you circled? Explain feelings and actions which relate. Be prepared to share your thoughts in this week's group session.**

_____

_____

_____

_____

✎ **Write a prayer thanking God or asking for His help in relationship to your stage in the grief recovery process.**

_____

_____

_____

_____

_____

# DAY 3

# Resolving Suffering

*Then she [Naomi] said, "Behold, your sister-in-law has gone back to her people and her gods; return after your sister-in-law." But Ruth said, "Do not urge me to leave you or turn back from following you; for where you go, I will go, and where you lodge, I will lodge. Your people shall be my people and your God, my God. Where you die, I will die, and there I will be buried. Thus may the Lord do to me, and worse, if anything but death parts you and me."*

—Ruth 1:15-17

Ruth must not have heard the adage about marrying your spouse and not your in-laws. When she married Naomi's son, she also made a commitment to her husband's family, his homeland, and his God. In effect, she told Naomi, "I can't go back. When I married your son, I married you, and I married your God. You're stuck with me—both in this life and in the life to come, because even death will not separate us."

Ruth knew that her commitment had changed who she was and that she could not return to her old life. Ruth was grieving too. Her husband was dead, and she had no children. But even in her suffering, she knew her future lay with Naomi and with Naomi's God. She had pulled up the roots of the past and committed herself to the future. So Naomi and Ruth journeyed to a city called Bethlehem. When they arrived, Naomi's feelings had not changed. She was as bitter and angry as she had been when she left Moab. She still did not realize what God had planned for her.

The rest of the book tells how Ruth marries and has a son. Naomi's friends speak to Naomi the words appearing in the margin. Naomi's life certainly did not play out the way she had planned, but tremendous blessing came out of her loss and grief. She thought her life was empty, but God gave her a daughter-in-law who was better to her than seven sons. God gave her all she needed to begin again. He also used her new beginning to bless all generations which followed. Ruth's son, Obed, was an ancestor of King David and of the promised Messiah, Jesus Christ. What a blessing! And Naomi was part of it. But the blessing grew out of suffering and the loss of her husband and her sons.

*"Blessed is the Lord. ... May [This child] also be to you a restorer of life and a sustainer of your old age; for your daughter-in-law, who loves you and is better to you than seven sons, has given birth to him."*
*—Ruth 4:14-15*

✎ **Are you grieving over the death of a person or some loss? Explain.**

_____

_____

✎ **What are your feelings about that loss?**

_____

_____

*Only God knows what He desires to do with your suffering and grief.*

Only God knows what He desires to do with your suffering and grief—whether it relates to tobacco or some other loss or change. Your decision of faith is to trust God even when you cannot see the outcome. However, faith is not always easy, and it usually is difficult to see any good in suffering. No healthy person ever feels good about suffering; pain is never enjoyable. If you have a vision of the future which brings you courage, be thankful.

➤ **If you are still in too much grief to look forward to the future, consider the following lessons from Naomi. Check those lessons you will seek to apply to your life this week.**

❑ Admit and express your feelings to yourself, to God, and to your support system.
❑ Make choices and changes. Do not allow grief to immobilize you. Naomi returned home. You may need to make some choices and changes as well.
❑ Count your blessings. Perhaps God has placed a spiritual "Ruth" in your life. Look for that person.
❑ Realize that someone is depending on you. Ruth turned to Naomi as a role model for her faith. Although human, Naomi did not fail Ruth.
❑ Wait. It's the most difficult lesson of all, and God frequently asks us to learn to do it. God's will and timetable are perfect for your life. Don't rush God.

➤ Take time to talk with God. Share with God your gratitude for all the good things and people in your life.

*Father, Your Word says in 1 Peter 5:6-7, "Humble yourselves, therefore, under the mighty hand of God, that He may exalt you at the proper time, casting all your anxiety upon Him, because He cares for you." That is what I am doing right now. I humble myself under Your will for my life. I give You each of my worries and concerns and trust You to take care of me. Thank You for my many blessings. Give me a heart of gratitude. Amen.*

➤ Review Isaiah 53:5 and your other Scripture memory verses.

# Forgiving Others

*He [Jesus] was despised and forsaken of men; A man of sorrows, and acquainted with grief; And like one from whom men hide their face, He was despised, and we did not esteem Him. Surely our griefs He Himself bore, And our sorrows He carried; Yet we ourselves esteemed Him stricken, Smitten of God, and afflicted. But He was pierced for our transgressions, He was crushed for our iniquities; The chastening for our well-being fell upon Him, And by his scourging we are healed.*

—Isaiah 53:3-5

Sometimes we focus so intensely on the problems of our own lives that we overlook the suffering of others. We forget that God's hand guards and protects His children. We fail to remember that God works in every situation to bring about good for us. If we are not careful, we become resistant to change and resentful of losses. We allow stressful relationships and situations to turn us into doubting, unforgiving people.

*We allow situations to turn us into doubting, unforgiving people.*

No one gets through life without grief. In the stress of family and work, we experience abuse and hurt. If we are not careful, we begin keeping score, counting all the injustices we have experienced. We can count the small everyday hurts as well as the major abuses. You may have been abused or neglected by a parent. You may have a family member who never has anything good to say about you. You may have an unreasonable boss or co-worker. You may even have been hurt by a person in a church. The negative emotions which relate to these hurts can keep you from recovery and the abundant life Christ desires to give you.

✎ Are there hurtful persons or situations in your past or present which have power over you? Describe each. Use additional paper as needed.

_____

_____

_____

_____

_____

Review today's Scripture. Ponder the beauty of the words. Jesus carried our grief and sorrows. He suffered for our iniquities. His punishment offers us wholeness. The word *whole* means *completeness*. If you have the whole thing, you have all there is. Nothing is lacking. No part is missing. It is finished—complete—entire. Wholeness is the beauty of the abundant life offered by Christ when He becomes Lord or Boss of our lives.

## Reframing Your View of Past Hurts

Suffering is a part of the complete life. Suffering teaches you to trust God. When you face problems too great for your own strength, you learn to trust God. You can reframe your view of the past hurts or abuses you have suffered. You can choose to see them as part of God's plan for your life. You can say: "That this happened was not necessarily good or what God would have chosen for me, but God is greater than the circumstances. He can use the circumstances of my life to build my character."

*God can use the circumstances of my life to build my character.*

You can forgive the people who hurt you. You can give up your desire for revenge. You can release your justifiable feelings of anger. You cannot cling to old negative attitudes and live the life of recovery. Forgiveness is difficult. In fact, forgiveness is sometimes humanly impossible. In your human strength to forgive absolutely an abusive parent or spouse seems impossible. But surrendering your will to the power and peace of God will bring forgiveness. If you do not forgive those who hurt you, you hold yourself in bondage. Unforgiveness will be a stumbling block to your recovery.

✎ **In the following paragraph underline clues that indicate how Jesus was able to avoid bitterness over the injustices He suffered. Then write an application statement describing how you can do the same.**

Jesus was a "man of sorrows and acquainted with grief" (Isaiah 53:3). The sorrows and grief which Christ bore were not His own; they were yours and mine. Unlike us, Christ did not have to submit to the abuses of any human, earthly power, or spiritual being. Christ had all of the power of God at His disposal. Yet Scripture describes Him as a "man of sorrows." Why would anyone choose to suffer if it could be avoided? There is only one answer—love. Christ loved you so much that He chose to suffer so that you would not have to. That's why you can call Him Savior. That is why you can trust Him and call Him Lord.

*Christ loved you so much that He chose to suffer in your place.*

✎ **Below write an application statement describing how Jesus dealt with injustice and how you can follow His example.**

_____

_____

You may have underlined the phrases about Jesus suffering not His own griefs but ours and about His choosing to suffer so that you would not have to. You could have expanded that in your written answer by describing how Jesus chose to view His pain and suffering as worthwhile because He saw a greater purpose. Jesus reframed the situation like this: "I know the Father has a purpose for this. He will bring good from My suffering, therefore why should I allow bitterness to spoil what God is accomplishing?"

*If you do not forgive people who have hurt you, you cripple yourself.*

If you take a top athlete and tie one hand behind his or her back, that player will not be able to perform to expectations. In the same way, if you do not forgive people who have hurt you, you cripple yourself. You will not be able to live life effectively. If you forgive most circumstances but refuse to forgive one person or situation, you tie a spiritual arm behind yourself. You limit how you will understand God, and you limit His ability to bring His character into your life.

Forgiveness is seldom an event. It is not a one-time, pie-in-the-sky feeling of euphoria which strikes like a bolt of lightning and causes you to forget that you hurt. Forgiveness is a process which begins with a decision. You cannot do the work of forgiveness in one moment or in one day, but you can begin the journey by taking the first step by turning loose of your own thoughts and feelings and giving God the right to be absolute Lord of your life. You can choose to trust God to deal with those persons who have abused or hurt you.

✎ **Do you know that God through Christ has forgiven you of each sin in your life?** ❏ Yes  ❏ No

✎ **Are there persons or events you need to forgive?** ❏ Yes  ❏ No

God has forgiven you. He is a forgiving God. To experience full recovery, you must take on this characteristic of God. You can begin by forgiving those who are a barrier to your abundant life. Consider the course map. You can continue to jump over the hurdles placed in your path by unloving people, or you can forgive. When you choose forgiveness, God removes the hurdle, smoothes your path, and makes the way clear.

➤ **Take time to pray about your need in the area of forgiveness.**

➤ **Attempt to write from memory your Scripture memory verse for this week. You may check your work on page 92.**

_____

_____

## DAY 5

# Loving the Way God Does

An old saying goes something like this: "If you stand too close to a grave, it will fill your world." When you stand up really close to anything, your peripheral vision is limited. The object you have your nose against fills your vision and keeps you from seeing other things around you. This is true spiritually as well as physically. You can allow a feeling, job, goal, person, or a situation to fill your mind. It can become the focus of your energy and time. It can fill your world. If you stand too close to grief, either the grief of giving up tobacco or some other loss, you will miss out on God's love and peace.

Right now you are standing close to your addiction to nicotine, and it probably fills most of your world. Recovery occupies a lot of your thoughts and feelings. Today, it is time for you to take another step away from your addiction. Turn loose of the past. Let go of your anger at addiction and yourself for being addicted. Forgive those who have hurt you. Forgive yourself for not being perfect. Step back and take a good look at the beauty of life and the future before you. Get your eyes off the past, and look forward. Take off those glasses of addiction through which you looked at the world, and put on spiritual glasses of God's love and forgiveness.

When you put on the glasses of love provided by God, it will change the way you understand people and situations. You will begin to take on the characteristics of God in your understanding of other people. First John 4:8, 16 say, "God is love." God does not have the characteristic of love. God *is* love. Love makes up His very being. God simply cannot be or do some things, because He is love.

✎ **First Corinthians 13:1-8 appears in the margin. In the passage, circle the characteristics of love, and underline the things that love is not.**

The characteristics you circled describe God. Those underlined are things God simply cannot be or do, because they are not characteristics of love. God cannot be arrogant or act unbecomingly; He cannot rejoice in wrongdoing.

➤ **Consider your understanding of God. Is your relationship with Him based on the characteristics of love? Are you, as His child, like Him in displaying the qualities of love?**

God wants you to be like Him. The more you allow the love of God in your life, the more you will see His characteristics in your relationships, and the less you will see the undesirable characteristics.

As you review work you have done this week about grief and loss, you may find the following suggestions helpful. Seek to take these actions when you feel overwhelmed with feelings of grief and loss.

1. **Identify feelings.** Try to understand their root causes.
2. **Express feelings.** Rather than hiding them, talk to a trusted friend, pastor, or counselor.
3. **Don't set a timetable for grief and healing.** To forgive and experience spiritual healing takes time.
4. **Build a personal support system.** People do exist who want to love, support and encourage you. Find them. Ask for their help. Give yours to them in return.
5. **Set daily achievable goals.** Work toward them. Even small tasks give purpose and a sense of accomplishment.
6. **Be cautious about resolving relationships.** A right time and way exists to approach a person with whom you have had a bad relationship. If talking will make the problem worse, don't do it. Writing a letter can provide an outlet for your feelings and give you opportunity to confront the person. The letter can then be shared in the confidentiality of your support group, with a trusted sponsor, or friend. You can then prayerfully decide to throw the letter away or to mail it.
7. **Trust God.** Each moment of your life is in God's care. Each hair of your head is numbered. God allows and brings good from even the painful events of your life. Your current grief or pain may not feel like a blessing, but God utilizes all things for good in the lives of His children.

If I speak with the tongues of men and of angels, but do not have love, I have become a noisy gong or a clanging cymbal. And if I have the gift of prophecy, and know all mysteries and all knowledge; and if I have all faith, so as to remove mountains, but do not have love, I am nothing. And if I give all my possessions to feed the poor, and if I deliver my body to be burned, but do not have love, it profits me nothing. Love is patient, love is kind, and is not jealous; love does not brag and is not arrogant, does not act unbecomingly; it does not seek its own, is not provoked, does not take into account a wrong suffered, does not rejoice in unrighteousness, but rejoices with the truth; bears all things, believes all things, hopes all things, endures all things. Love never fails.
—1 Corinthians 13:1-8

<table>
<tr><td>

**The most relevant steps for me—**

_____

_____

_____

_____

_____

_____

_____

</td><td>

✎ In the margin describe which of the previous steps are most relevant for you and why.

➤ Ask God to give you His love and forgiveness in all your relationships.

✎ On a separate sheet of paper write a good-bye letter to tobacco. Below I have provided you a sample, but your letter should contain your personal thoughts and feelings. If you are not ready to write a goodbye letter, write a letter expressing your feelings about tobacco. Later, when you are ready, write a good-bye letter to tobacco. Be prepared to share your letter in this week's support group session.

</td></tr>
</table>

*Dear Cigarettes (or Brand),*
*For me to say good-bye is difficult. We've been friends for many years, and you have helped me through a lot of difficult times. Now I realize that you were not the friend I thought you were; you were a false friend. The entire time I thought you were helping me, you were really hurting me. When I think about how easily you trapped me, I feel angry. I have only myself to blame. I chose to give you power over my life and to spend time with you instead of with my family and friends. I chose to spend my money on you instead of using it in productive ways and to give you control over my body and health. But that is over now. I am finished with you—forever. I have forgiven myself and have asked God to forgive me. The future is ahead of me, and you are not part of it. I am going to live in a new way—without you.*
                                          *Good-bye,*
                                          *(Name)*

## Preparing for Your Support Group Session

As you prepare for your support-group meeting, review the following areas of this week's work.

1. List the losses you have experienced in your life. Be prepared to share how you have or have not grieved the losses.
2. Be prepared to share how you relate to the stages of grief in your tobacco use and in your recovery from tobacco addiction.
3. If hurtful persons or situations in your past or present continue to have power over you, share your plan for dealing with your hurt, fear, and anger.
4. Review the 7 suggested actions on page 102 for processing grief.

———————

Notes
[1]Kubler-Ross, Elisabeth, *On Death and Dying,* (New York: Macmillan Publishing Co. Inc., 1969).

# Finishing the Race

## HOW CAN I SUPPORT YOU?

Chris and Marie had been married for 15 years when Chris decided to quit smoking. Marie had never smoked, so she could not understand how difficult recovery was for Chris. She wanted to help but often did not know how. When she asked Chris how he was doing, he usually responded with a terse reply that let her know he felt that Marie was checking up on him. But she felt guilty when she didn't ask, because she didn't want him to think she didn't care. Marie worried most on the evenings Chris went to his bowling league. Most of the bowlers were smokers, and she was afraid Chris would succumb to temptation. He always smelled strongly of cigarette smoke when he came home, and it scared Marie. She wanted to trust Chris, but she had a small nagging doubt that he might fail this time just as he had in the past.

Finally, Marie decided she would talk to Chris about her feelings. She waited until they were eating out one evening, and Chris seemed open and relaxed. Marie said, "Chris, I want you to know how proud I am of you for not smoking. I know it has been difficult. I want to help but don't know how. Does it bother you when I ask if you are doing OK, or do you feel I am checking up on you? I would really appreciate knowing how to encourage you."

**What you'll learn**

This week you will—
- perceive the abundant life of recovery as a way of thinking and acting rather than a one-time event;
- reaffirm your understanding that no cure for addiction exists—you must rely on God rather than living in your own strength;
- review issues which might cause you to leave your recovery half finished;
- learn the difference between a slip and a lapse and identify thoughts which can lead to relapse;
- evaluate your urge to use tobacco and identify potential situations which could jeopardize your recovery and cause you to relapse.

**What you'll study**

| Abundant Living Is a Process | Stay on the Road | Finishing What You've Started | Encouragement | Evaluate Your Progress |
|---|---|---|---|---|
| DAY 1 | DAY 2 | DAY 3 | DAY 4 | DAY 5 |

This week's passage of Scripture to memorize—

**Memory verse**

*He [Jesus] could do no miracle there except that He laid His hands upon a few sick people and healed them. And He wondered at their unbelief.*

—Mark 6:5-6

<table>
<tr>
<td>

**DAY**

**1**

</td>
<td>

# Abundant Living Is a Process

Mark 6:45-52 tells how Jesus *made* His disciples get into a boat and go ahead of Him across the sea of Galilee. Jesus used the time alone to pray. Then He walked across the sea to meet the disciples on the other side. In the margin read Mark 6:49-52—the disciples' reaction when they saw Jesus.

</td>
</tr>
</table>

When they saw Him walking on the sea, they supposed that it was a ghost, and cried out; for they all saw Him and were frightened. But immediately He spoke with them and said to them, "Take courage; it is I; do not be afraid." And He got into the boat with them, and the wind stopped; and they were greatly astonished, for they had not gained any insight from the incident of the loaves, but their heart was hardened.

—Mark 6:49-52

He [Jesus] could do no miracle there except that He laid His hands upon a few sick people and healed them. And He wondered at their unbelief.

—Mark 6:5-6

The disciples did what Jesus instructed and rowed straight into a sea of distress which threatened their lives. When He noticed their problem, Jesus set out walking on the water toward them. But instead of stopping and helping them, He intended to "pass them by." The disciples had spent time listening to Jesus teach that He was the only Son of the one true living God. They had seen His miracles, but they still did not know Jesus had absolute control over everything in heaven and on earth.

Mark 6:5 suggests that the people's unbelief limited the power of Jesus to do miracles. Apparently God chooses to respect humans so much that He even allows our unbelief to limit His actions. Yet even when we doubt, like the disciples, God still responds to our distress. We may feel we are alone in the boat of recovery, struggling against adverse winds which seem too powerful for us to overcome. In reality, Jesus is walking in the storm with us; He just may allow us to fight our battles in our own strength until we learn to trust Him. If we reach out, He can get into the boat with us and calm the storm.

## Spiritual Health During Maintenance

I wish I could sit down with you personally and ask how your recovery from nicotine dependence is going. Your response might be positive and filled with wonderful stories of how you are coping with daily or unexpected challenges. Or perhaps your recovery is not going well, and you are tempted to give up and turn back. If so remember, whatever your personal storm, no matter how small your boat, Jesus can join you and still your storm. No matter how frightened you are, Jesus can calm your fears and bring His peace to your life.

Wanting Jesus in your life, however, is not the same as wanting the things Jesus can do for you. Sometimes, we want Jesus to be our personal magician, a kind of magic genie, who comes at our bidding and grants our wishes. We want Him to fix this or take care of that, but we do not really want Him in every part of our lives. We certainly do not want Jesus to be Lord of every area of life. The problem with this kind of thinking is that we attempt to surrender certain parts of life to Him while we keep the rest under our own control.

Jesus will not have that kind of relationship with anyone. He does not enter into spiritual partnerships. Jesus will not reach out a steadying hand when the boat of your life rocks in heavy waves. He will not magically move your boat to safe ground. What Jesus will do is get into the boat with you.

✎ **In your recovery thus far, which kind of relationship have you had with Jesus Christ?**

❏ I have thought of Jesus as a magician who could grant my wishes.
❏ I have focused on giving Jesus full control in my life.

**In your own words, define the difference in wanting Jesus and in wanting the things Jesus can do for you.**

_____

_____

**Trust—no matter what**

You need the attitude which gives Jesus Christ full authority as Lord or Boss of your life if you are to experience the full abundant life. Without this kind of faith, the power of Jesus Christ will not fully express itself in your life. Jesus will not perform the miracles He desires unless you choose to trust Him—no matter what.

As you enter this final stage called Maintenance, remember that recovery is a process. The abundant life of recovery is not a location or an attitude which you can once achieve and then sit back and do nothing. Jesus may have entered your life and calmed the storm, but you are still in the boat at sea. You will experience other storms to weather, but you are not alone.

When you initially thought about giving up tobacco, perhaps you did not know it would be the beginning of a spiritual journey for you. Hopefully these past weeks have helped you understand God in a new way and taught you to rely on Him in each situation.

He [Jesus] could do no miracle there except that He laid His hands upon a few sick people and healed them. And He wondered at their unbelief.

—Mark 6:5-6

 **Begin to memorize Mark 6:5-6, your Scripture memory verses for this week. Write the verses on a card to carry with you. Repeat the verses throughout the day.**

# Stay on the Road

**DAY 2**

The course map compares recovery to running a race. Some people begin the race of recovery well. They run well and do all the right things. Then along the road, they get distracted by some person or situation. They lose their concentration and their focus on the goal of abundant life. When that happens, they turn aside from the race. It can happen to anyone. It can happen to you. Scripture tells a curious story about a prophet named Balaam who represents a useful illustration.

The King of Moab attempted to hire Balaam to curse the Israelites, but God clearly told Balaam not to go with the king's messengers. Like a child who wants something and refuses to take no for an answer, Balaam asked God a second time, so God allowed him to go. On the trip Balaam was riding his donkey. Three times the angel of the Lord blocked their path. Each time the donkey saw the angel, refused to go forward, and thereby saved Balaam's life. Each time Balaam beat the donkey. Finally God spoke to Balaam through the donkey. The result was the only talking donkey in history. After the donkey spoke, God opened Balaam's eyes to see the angel of the Lord. Read the words of the angel appearing in the margin.

The angel of the Lord asked him, "Why have you beaten your donkey these three times? I have come here to oppose you because your path is a reckless one before me. The donkey saw me and turned away from me these three times. If she had not turned away, I would certainly have killed you by now, but I would have spared her."

–Numbers 22:32-33, NIV

Balaam started out with the right attitude. He did what God said—until he got an offer he couldn't resist. Perhaps Balaam's intentions were good in his own eyes, but God became angry when Balaam decided to do what the king wanted instead of what God had told him to do. Balaam could have avoided a lot of trouble by thinking ahead and staying on the road God had planned for him. The same thing is true in recovery. You can choose to stay on the road of recovery, or you can go off on your own paths.

Thinking about situations which might cause you to relapse is part of staying on the road of recovery. Some people do not want to think about the risk of relapse. They are confident that they will never relapse—that it simply cannot happen to them. The facts show that relapse can happen to anyone. Unlike Balaam, we cannot count on a donkey and an angel to turn us aside from danger. The best way to avoid a pothole in the road is to know where it is. The best way to avoid relapse is to know the dangerous pitfalls and plan to avoid them.

*The best way to avoid a pothole is to know where it is.*

## No Cure for Addiction

The first thing you must know is that you are not cured of nicotine addiction. No cure for addiction exists. Your addiction is dormant because you are not using tobacco. It no longer controls your thinking, feelings, and actions, but the potential is still there. Many professionals think this potential for relapse is physically based. They think that people who use even a small amount of the drug they were addicted to in the past are vulnerable to relapse. A person who has been abstinent for weeks or months may decide to have "just one." That one cigarette or chew leads to another, then to occasional use, and then to relapse to the amount previously used—or perhaps even more.

You cannot afford to deceive yourself by thinking you are cured. You have to accept that just one puff or chew may make you vulnerable to relapse. Addicts of all kinds have tried and failed until they understood that they could not control their use of the substance. It is true that some persons can be social smokers, but you are not one of them.

You could spend lots of emotional energy arguing that *it's not fair* or asking *why me?* But that kind of thinking is futile. It is much more productive to use your energy to face the problem and make plans to avoid relapse.

## Physical Health During Maintenance

If you chose nicotine replacement therapy to minimize withdrawal symptoms, you may have already begun tapering or reducing the amount of nicotine you have been receiving. If you have not begun to taper, you should now set a date for when you will begin. A tapering schedule should be determined under the advice of your physician or counselor. After you have been abstinent from tobacco four to six weeks, you may be ready to taper your use of nicotine. A suggestion is that you set a date within the next two weeks, then taper at two to three week intervals in order to be off all forms of nicotine within the next four to six weeks.

**Time to taper**

Use the emotional, spiritual, and mental coping skills you have learned to offset the minimal withdrawal you will experience as you decrease your dose of nicotine replacement.

If you are smoking or using any other form of tobacco while on nicotine replacement therapy, you are particularly vulnerable to relapse. Three alternatives are available to you:

1. Discontinue prescription nicotine therapy and return to tobacco use until you are more motivated for abstinence.
2. Discuss your medication with your physician to determine if you need a higher replacement dosage.
3. Decide you are going to discontinue all lapses immediately. Take an honest look at why you are allowing yourself occasional uses of tobacco.

**Doing exceedingly well**

If you are not currently on any form of nicotine and are not having any lapses, you are doing exceedingly well. Although your body has not fully returned to its normal healthy state, you are well on the road to recovery. Your greatest risk of relapse from this point relates to emotional, social, or spiritual issues rather than physical ones.

## Psychological Health During Maintenance

Many persons who relapse after several weeks, months, or even years of abstinence do so for emotional reasons. In the past few weeks, you have begun to learn about your emotions. You have begun to recognize them and found ways of coping with them. You may still be uncomfortable with some feelings because you hid from them for so many years behind tobacco use. For example, you may still have difficulty coping with anger or communicating your feelings. It takes time to relearn ways of coping with emotions.

✎ **How is your physical recovery from nicotine dependence going?**

_____

_____

✎ **What changes, if any, will you make during the next few weeks?**

_____

_____

✎ **What problems are you experiencing in your emotional recovery plan?**

_____

_____

✎ **What are you feeling as you think about your support group ending?**

_____

_____

✎ **Do you need the encouragement and accountability of an ongoing support group?** ❑ Yes ❑ No

➤ Take time to pray. Tell God about your feelings today.

➤ Review Mark 6:5-6, your Scripture memory verses for this unit.

<table>
<tr><td>

# DAY 3

</td><td>

# Finishing What You've Started

</td></tr>
</table>

Gary asked his support group to pray for him. He said, "I have been off smokeless tobacco since we started this group eight weeks ago. All that time, I have been using nicotine gum to help me cope with the urge to chew. I've been averaging about 12 pieces of nicotine gum each day, but tomorrow I am going to begin cutting back. My doctor said I should use 11 pieces each day this week, 10 each day the next week, and so on until I am totally off the gum. I agreed with her, but I'm nervous. I have relied on the gum to get me over the rough spots. I just want you to say an extra prayer for me this week. It's important that I finish what I've started and not become dependent on the nicotine gum."

*Ephraim has become a cake not turned.*
*—Hosea 7:8*

Gary was committed to finishing what he had started. He was not like God's people, who initially followed the will of God but then turned aside and went their own way. God says their actions were like a "cake not turned." A pancake cooked on one side but left raw on the other is unappetizing; it will not bring much pleasure to the person who hopes to eat it. Everyone fails to finish a project at some time. By making plans to finish your recovery from nicotine dependence, you can complete the work of recovery rather than leaving it half done.

## Interpersonal Health During Maintenance

The weeks and months ahead will bring challenges and temptations. Lapses can happen, but you can avoid them. Feelings and situations reported by former tobacco users to be most challenging are those which have to do with social situations or conflict with other people.

 **The following list contains situations which contribute to relapse. To rate the degree that each situation tends to cause you difficulty, mark each with either an *H* for high, *M* for medium, or *L* for low degree of difficulty.**

**Contributors to relapse**

\_\_\_\_ Intense emotions—either negative or positive
\_\_\_\_ Conflict with another person
\_\_\_\_ Holidays and celebrations
\_\_\_\_ Feeling deprived or that I am missing out by not using tobacco
\_\_\_\_ Unexpected or long-term stressful situations
\_\_\_\_ Becoming overconfident; thinking that nothing could ever make me use tobacco again
\_\_\_\_ Failure to work at recovery by changing attitudes and actions
\_\_\_\_ Giving myself permission to lapse once or occasionally under certain circumstances

Don't be disturbed if certain situations are difficult for you. Everyone is vulnerable during the entire first year of abstinence. Coping with holidays or other events resemble what a person experiences after the death of a loved one. You may feel uncomfortable the first time you celebrate Christmas, other holidays, or special events without tobacco. Once you have gone through each of these experiences, you will find it easier next time. As time passes, your urge to use tobacco will be less intense and less frequent.

The key lies in not dwelling on the past but in moving quickly away from thoughts of smoking or using tobacco. You cannot avoid thinking about tobacco and will occasionally miss using. You may even dream about using. These are not causes for concern. You are in danger only if you intentionally begin toying with the thought of using. To dismiss immediately any thoughts involving tobacco from your mind is better than to dwell on them.

## Coping with a Lapse

Hopefully, you will not need to know how to cope with a lapse to tobacco use, but the following suggestions will help if you ever need them. Refer to this list if you ever need it.

1. Where were you when the lapse occurred?
2. Who were you with?
3. What were you doing?
4. What were your feelings?
5. Was your lapse the result of a spontaneous impulse or had you been thinking about using tobacco for some time?
6. Where did you get the tobacco?
7. How much tobacco did you use?
8. Remind yourself that this is a one-time event. It changes nothing. Your goal is still abstinence.
9. Get rid of all tobacco immediately.
10. As soon as possible, talk with someone about your lapse. Make a personal and a verbal commitment to begin working your program immediately.

Each of the questions is important to understand what was happening and how you were feeling at the time the lapse occurred. You may find that being with a certain person or in a specific location challenges your recovery. If you have used tobacco even once during recovery thus far, answer the previous questions. Share this experience with your support group if you have not already done so.

✎ **If you have had lapses during your recovery, what types of circumstances or feelings have made abstinence difficult?**

_____

_____

✎ **Do you tend to think in extreme, *all or nothing*, terms? ❏ Yes  ❏ No**
**If so, begin changing your thought pattern to accept that a slip does not mean that you are powerless to control your future recovery.**

✎ **If you ever are strongly tempted to use tobacco, who would you talk to about the temptation?**

_____

*A wise person does not run in front of speeding cars.*

Finally, do not set yourself up to fail. Although you know that some persons have lapsed, to use tobacco even once is a dangerous thing. A wise person does not run in front of speeding cars. A wise ex-tobacco user does not toy with nicotine use.

# Encouragement

When Brad stopped using tobacco, he asked his best friend, Pete, if he would agree to be his support person. Pete agreed. During the next six weeks, Brad relied on Pete on several occasions. Since they worked together they could talk during work breaks about Brad's progress. On difficult days when Brad wondered if he was going to make it, Pete always helped restore Brad's perspective.

One of the early disciples called Barnabas was an encourager. In fact, his real name was Joseph (Acts 4:36), but the disciples had nicknamed him Barnabas which means "The Encourager." When Paul turned from persecuting and killing Christians to faith in Jesus Christ, it was Barnabas who supported him. Other believers were afraid to trust that Paul had changed, but Barnabas encouraged them to trust him.

Paul and Barnabas then became co-workers who traveled and preached together. Eventually, they decided to return to some of the cities where they had established churches and encourage the believers. Then Paul and Barnabas argued over whether to take John Mark with them. Barnabas was a man who believed in giving people a chance to start over. Paul was not willing to take John Mark, because he had abandoned them on a previous trip. Paul and Barnabas wound up going in different directions, and Barnabas took John Mark with him. Later, the conflict was resolved, and Paul included John Mark in the ministry. The result of Barnabas' encouragement was the growth and maturity of John Mark.

> Barnabas wanted to take John, also called Mark, with them, but Paul did not think it wise to take him, because he had deserted them in Pamphylia and had not continued with them in the work. They had such a sharp disagreement that they parted company.
>
> —Acts 15:37-39, NIV

All of us need the encouragement and support of other people. You have realized this as you made changes necessary to maintain abstinence from tobacco. Perhaps the words of a member of your group encouraged you. Maybe you found hope for your own recovery in the example of another addicted person. To make changes in your routines and beliefs is not easy, but you are doing it. The strength and encouragement of God, friends, family, and your support group have helped bring you this far. As you set goals for the weeks ahead, do not neglect your need for encouragement.

## Accountability

You cannot always count on someone else being present at the exact moment you are tempted. The real struggle of recovery is to be personally accountable for your choices. One way to practice accountability is by examining the words you use—and possibly the excuses you make.

✎ **Write your own definition for the following words.**

Slip _____

Lapse_____

Relapse _____

Sometimes people who are recovering say they slip when they have been abstinent and then smoke a cigarette or use tobacco. It is better to call this type of situation a lapse rather than a slip. The word *slip* implies that the person had no control over the event. People slip when they are walking on ice or hit a slick spot on the floor. Although this can happen in tobacco use, most of the time it is not the reality of what happens. Many times, lapses occur when a person sets up a situation with the intention of using. This may be a subconscious or a conscious choice.

If you slip on a slick spot on the sidewalk, you may fall. However, the next time you come down that sidewalk on an icy day, you will remember the slick spot and watch out for it. If you continue to take the same slippery route and fall down in the same slick spot day after day, you are accountable. Accountability means learning from mistakes and avoiding them in the future.

*If you continue to take the same slippery route, you are accountable.*

✎ **Do you agree that a lapse is usually a personal choice rather than an accident?** ❑ **Yes** ❑ **No  Explain your answer.**

_____

_____

✎ **What does your attitude have to do with your actions?**

_____

_____

✎ **When the group ends, what method of accountability will you use?**

_____

_____

✎ **Write a prayer expressing to God your feelings and intentions about accountability.**

_____

_____

_____

✎ **In the margin attempt to write Mark 6:5-6 from memory. Check your work on page 105. Continue to memorize and review your memory verses.**

## DAY 5

# Evaluate Your Progress

Chris and Marie had been married for 15 years when Chris decided to quit smoking. Marie had never smoked, so she could not understand how difficult recovery was for Chris. She wanted to help but often did not know how. When she asked Chris how he was doing, he usually responded with a terse reply that let her know he felt that she was checking up on him. But she felt guilty when she didn't ask, because she didn't want him to think she didn't care. Marie worried most on the evenings Chris went to his bowling league. Most of the bowlers were smokers, and she was afraid Chris would succumb to temptation. He always smelled strongly of cigarette smoke when he came home, and it scared Marie. She wanted to trust Chris, but she had a small nagging doubt that he might fail this time just as he had in the past. Finally, Marie decided she would talk to Chris about her feelings. She waited until they were eating out one evening, and Chris seemed open and relaxed. Marie said, "Chris, I want you to know how proud I am of you for not smoking. I know it has been difficult. I want to help but don't know how. Does it bother you when I ask if you are doing OK, or do you feel I am checking up on you? I would really appreciate knowing how to encourage you."

Marie's words were what Chris needed. He started talking about his recovery—about things that were going well and about his struggles. As they talked, they agreed on some things Marie could do that Chris would find helpful. They also agreed on some things she would stop doing. Both realized they needed to talk more about Chris' recovery. They set a date for the next weekend when they would again go out together and talk.

## The Nature of Addiction

Tobacco did not exist in ancient Israel, but Hosea's words appearing at left could just as well have been spoken describing addiction to nicotine. Addiction is bottomless. No amount of nicotine, alcohol, food, chemical, or compulsive action is ever enough. Being addicted is like putting your life into a bag with holes in it. Anyone who continues in addiction will eventually watch their blessings run through those holes in the bottom of the bag of life. Nicotine addiction already may have caused some of your blessings to be lost: health, money, self-respect, time, or relationships. You may not be able to recapture what has been lost, but you can choose not to lose any more. Christ can mend the holes of vulnerability in your bag of life.

✎ **Describe the kind of situations most likely to tempt you to lapse.**

| Situations which could cause me to lapse | Ways I can avoid a lapse |
| --- | --- |
| _____ | _____ |
| _____ | _____ |
| _____ | _____ |
| _____ | _____ |
| _____ | _____ |
| _____ | _____ |

If you did not include types of thoughts which could tempt you to lapse, go back and add them to the chart. Examples might be thoughts such as the following:
- I can surely smoke just one after all this time.
- If I smoke just one, I will get this preoccupation out of my system and get on with my program.
- I am missing out on so much by not using tobacco.

Honest communications

Now therefore, thus says the LORD of hosts, "Consider your ways! You have sown much, but harvest little; you eat, but there is not enough to be satisfied; you drink, but there is not enough to become drunk; you put on clothing, but no one is warm enough; and he who earns, earns wages to put into a purse with holes.

—Haggai 1:5-6

- I'm not going to make it anyway, I might as well give up now.
- I'll just smoke or use tobacco until this crisis is over; then I'll stop again.

Evaluate your responses on the previous chart. Are you more vulnerable in certain types of situations? Perhaps stress or other feelings are your biggest challenge. If you do not see any pattern in your response or are concerned about a specific item, share it with your group this week.

## Evaluating Your Urge to Use

✎ Complete the following to review your progress in managing cues to lapse.

1. On an average, how many times a day/week do you feel an urge to use tobacco? _____
2. On an average, how strong are these urges?
   ❑ Mild          ❑ Moderate          ❑ Strong

✎ 3. When do you experience these urges? Check all that apply.

**Understanding the urges**

❑ When I feel bored, lonely, or depressed.
❑ When I am tired or overworked.
❑ When I am with a person who uses tobacco.
❑ In the morning as I start my day.
❑ In the evening when I am relaxing.
❑ When I am angry or anxious.
❑ When I am having a good time.
❑ After or while eating a meal or snack.
❑ They come out of the blue and don't appear to be associated with any particular person or event.

❑ Other: _____
❑ Other: _____

✎ 4. What coping methods have you tried which worked in each situation? Write your response after each phrase above.

**Choosing personal rewards**

✎ Rewarding yourself for even small positive changes is an important part of working your recovery program. What rewards have you given yourself?

❑ Treated myself to personal time, either alone or doing an enjoyable activity.
❑ Bought myself something with money saved by not using tobacco.
❑ Gave myself a personal "pat on the back" for sticking with abstinence.
❑ Reminded myself of the positive changes in my health from not using tobacco.
❑ Told someone about my recovery program.

❑ Other: _____
❑ Other: _____

**My motivations—**

_____

_____

_____

_____

✎ In the margin describe your primary motivations for continuing your recovery program at this time.

## Living Without Fear

I'm a creature of habit and usually take the same route on my morning walk. At one house, there is an old dog who likes to bark at me. Occasionally I am lost in thought, and he takes me by surprise. For just a second, his bark frightens me, and I get a rush of adrenaline remembering an experience years ago when a dog did attack me. But this dog is no cause for alarm—aged, toothless, and able to walk only feebly, he still likes to maintain his image by barking.

*You thought addiction would have you for the rest of your life.*

When you first stopped using tobacco, it was normal to be fearful—to wonder if you were strong enough to break the bonds of your addiction. You thought the dog of addiction would have you in its jaws for the rest of your life. But that was not true. As you continued one day at a time in the strength of God, little by little you weakened the hold of addiction.

In the future when you think about using tobacco, you may give a small jump of alarm—like I do when that old dog surprises me—but like that dog, your addiction will have lost its teeth and strength; it will have no power over you.

**Powerless over me**

When I hear of someone who has relapsed to smoking after months or years of being smoke-free, I am sad for them. But I am no longer afraid that the same will happen to me. I have no intention of going over to that old dog and letting it gum me to death. I see addiction for what it is, and it is powerless over me as long as I stay in Christ.

✎ **Do you know persons who have been in recovery from nicotine addiction or another chemical dependence for several years? Write their names.**

_____

_____

✎ **In your opinion, what changes in attitudes or actions have these persons made in order to maintain their abstinence?**

_____

_____

✎ **What is your personal vision for your future?**

_____

_____

_____

✎ **Turn to the course map. Place an *X* to show where you are in the process of recovery.**

➤ **Pray today thanking God that you can depend on His strength during your recovery process. Ask God to make clear to you His vision for your future. Include in your prayer persons you know who are in recovery.**

# Resisting Temptation: Planning for Maintenance

**Growth Goal:**
You will evaluate current high-risk circumstances and plan for the maintenance stage of recovery.

## PREPARING FOR THE STRESS

"My name is Kenny. I come from a large family, and we don't get along too well, but my wife and I live 600 miles away, so it isn't usually a problem. We're going back to my home state for Christmas. Being with my family always is difficult, and I am worried about going to visit. In the past when my family got together, I spent most of the time on the porch smoking. It was the perfect excuse to stay out of the turmoil and not get involved.

"One brother and I have always been close, and he's a smoker too. So we spend some quality time sitting together on the porch or walking around. I haven't seen him or any of my family since I quit smoking, and I don't know whether I can cope with the stress of being with them. I haven't even told any of them that I've quit smoking. It's going to be difficult to sit on the porch with my brother while he smokes and not have a cigarette with him. But it would be even more difficult to stay in the house all the time. I've thought about the situation a lot but still haven't come up with a plan for what to do."

**What you'll learn**

This week you will—
• identify personal situations and feelings which represent high risk for relapse and which cause you to stumble in your recovery;
• be asked to commit to building a deeper relationship with God as Lord of your life through Bible study, prayer, and worship;
• understand the role between attitude and action in continuing the progress of recovery;
• note positive changes in yourself and group members which reflect a different identity;
• begin turning loose of the strength of your support group and begin building a different support system.

**What you'll study**

| Coping with Stumbling Blocks | Build Relationships with God | Set and Achieve New Goals | A New Name, A New Start | Where Do You Go From Here? |
|---|---|---|---|---|
| DAY 1 | DAY 2 | DAY 3 | DAY 4 | DAY 5 |

This week's passage of Scripture to memorize—

**Memory verse**
*Because Thy lovingkindness is better than life, My lips will praise Thee.*
—Psalm 63:3

# Coping with Stumbling Blocks

✎ You read in the unit story about Kenny and the stressful situation he faced as he prepared to travel home for Christmas. What suggestions do you have for Kenny to help him cope with this situation?

_____

_____

✎ Describe any similar concerns about situations which could cause you to stumble.

_____

_____

Philip found Nathanael and said to him, "We have found Him of whom Moses in the Law and also the Prophets wrote, Jesus of Nazareth, the son of Joseph." And Nathanael said to him, "Can any good thing come out of Nazareth?" Philip said to him, "Come and see." Jesus saw Nathanael coming to Him, and said of him, "Behold, an Israelite indeed, in whom is no guile!" Nathanael said to Him, "How do you know me?" Jesus answered and said to him, "Before Philip called you, when you were under the fig tree, I saw you." Nathanael answered Him, "Rabbi, You are the Son of God; You are the King of Israel."

—John 1:45-49

John chapter one contains a story about a man named Nathanael. He had never met Jesus. When Philip told Nathanael about Jesus, he doubted Jesus could be the Messiah. His doubt was a stumbling block to faith. Nathanael could have chosen to refuse his brother's offer, but instead he went to meet Jesus.

I had a personal experience which reminded me of how easily I could stumble in my own recovery. My family and I were living at the time in Minnesota, and I was working as a counselor in an addiction program for smokers. One day, I was scheduled to see a patient whom I had previously counseled. She entered the room, sat down, pulled a pack of cigarettes out of her purse, and laid them on the table between us. She said, "Here, I want you to take these. I have been smoking again for the past week, and I am angry at myself for allowing this to happen. I do not want to be a smoker ever again. I want to give these cigarettes to you as part of my commitment to recovery."

From the moment she took the pack out of her purse and laid it on the table, I was in trouble. I doubt the patient even knew I was distracted. God and I were alone with my thoughts which went something like this: *Those cigarettes look wonderful. I sure would like one. In fact, I could smoke one and nobody would know. I could just slip them in my purse and smoke one on the drive home. No, I couldn't smoke in the car; my husband would smell the smoke and know I had been smoking. Maybe I could stop at the park; I see people smoking there all the time. No, someone who knows me might see me. If that happened, I would be looking for a new job…*

At about that point in my thinking, I realized how dangerous my fantasy was to my personal recovery. God alone knew how vulnerable I was in that moment, and I am positive the Spirit prayed for me when I was in too much crisis to pray for myself. When the patient left, I went down the hall looking for anyone with whom I could talk. One of the other counselors happened to be in, and we talked about my feelings.

As I talked, I realized that I had actually been toying with the idea of smoking for several weeks. I remembered thinking about buying a pack of cigarettes during a long drive several weeks earlier. My mother was terminally ill with bone cancer, and I had made several car trips by myself to my parents' home. The round trip was about 1,200 miles, and fatigue combined with the mental stress of knowing my mother was dying had brought me to the point of vulnerability. I remember thinking about buying cigarettes to help me stay awake during one long trip. I dismissed the thought, but it returned later when I was having difficulty coping with my grief over my mother's approaching death.

In a sense, my feelings of loss and physical fatigue resulted in a crisis the day the patient gave me her cigarettes. I wanted a way to escape the pain of my life, and the old patterns of my former addiction tempted me. As I talked through my feelings, I realized that what I really wanted was for my mother to live. Whether or not I smoked would have no impact on that, and remaining smoke-free was the better choice for me personally. This sounds logical now, but it was an intensely emotional struggle at the time.

This experience was the most significant temptation during my years of recovery. It was a strong warning, because I really thought there was no situation which could throw me off course after all these years.

✎ **Evaluate the story of my personal experience. What feelings were involved in my urge to smoke?**

_____

_____

✎ **Which thoughts made me vulnerable?**

_____

_____

✎ **Which thoughts helped me maintain recovery?**

_____

_____

✎ **What actions gave me strength to resist temptation?**

_____

_____

✎ **In what ways does this story trouble you?**

_____

_____

✎ **In what ways does this story offer you hope?**

_____

_____

In the above situation, grief and physical fatigue brought me to a low point where smoking appeared to be a way of escape. My distorted thoughts included thinking that a return to my addictive behavior would somehow bring comfort or relief. Fortunately, I recognized that I was in trouble and I talked with another person about what I was thinking and feeling. The very act of admitting my problem helped break the pull of the old addictive thoughts and feelings. I learned three lessons from the experience.

1. I am not invulnerable to relapse. Relapse can happen to anyone.
2. I am most vulnerable when I am tired and emotionally down.
3. Talking to a supportive person can provide focus and direction.

## Discovering Your Personal High Risks

Everyone has certain situations or feelings which are potential stumbling blocks to maintaining recovery. The circumstances most likely to cause you to lapse or relapse are your high risks. The following activity will help you understand your personal high risk situations or feelings. They are divided into the same four categories which you have used to organize your recovery plan so far. Add others as you work through each section.

✎ **In the following list, check the categories that increase your risk of relapse.**

**Physical hazards**
- ❏ Fatigue, simply not getting enough sleep and rest
- ❏ Eating certain foods
- ❏ Drinking specific beverages such as coffee or alcohol
- ❏ Other physical stumbling blocks: _____

**Psychological hazards**
- ❏ Intense negative feelings such as anger
- ❏ Feeling lonely
- ❏ Not enough personal time
- ❏ Intense positive feelings such as completion of a project
- ❏ Holidays, special events, or activities
- ❏ One particular time of the year, such as hunting or fishing season
- ❏ Other psychological stumbling blocks: _____

**Interpersonal hazards**
- ❏ Family celebrations
- ❏ Certain friends, family members, or acquaintances
- ❏ Social functions where others are using tobacco
- ❏ Not attending a 12-Step or other support group
- ❏ Other interpersonal stumbling blocks: _____

**Spiritual hazards**
- ❏ Lack of a regular time for Bible study and prayer
- ❏ Living in your own strength rather than trusting God
- ❏ Not worshiping with other believers regularly
- ❏ Other spiritual stumbling blocks: _____

✎ **Do any of the four categories have greater risk for you than others? Explain briefly.**

_____

_____

➤ If you are vulnerable in an area, pay more attention to personal growth in that area. Continue to use the weekly recovery plan sheet. Pay close attention to activities and attitudes which will make you stronger.

> *Lord God, I know that even when I am alone in my most private place, You too are there. When I, like Nathanael, am under my isolated "fig tree" and think no one sees me struggle and pray, You are there. Thank You for knowing the most secret thoughts and intents of my mind and yet loving me. Thank You for knowing who I really am, both the good and the bad, and yet loving me. Today, I again place my absolute trust in You and Your love for me. You alone know what difficulties lie ahead in my recovery. You alone can keep me strong and provide the answers I will need. Amen.*

✎ **Begin to memorize Psalm 63:3, your Scripture memory verse for this week. Write the verse on a card to carry with you then practice repeating the verse through the day.**

Because Thy lovingkindness is better than life, My lips will praise Thee.
—Psalm 63:3

## DAY 2

# Build Relationships with God

*O GOD, Thou art my God; I shall seek Thee earnestly; My soul thirsts for Thee, my flesh yearns for Thee, In a dry and weary land where there is no water.*

—Psalm 63:1

✎ **Have you ever felt you were in a "dry and weary land?"** ❏ Yes ❏ No **Explain briefly.**

_____

_____

Thus I have beheld Thee in the sanctuary, To see Thy power and Thy glory. Because Thy lovingkindness is better than life, My lips will praise Thee. So I will bless Thee as long as I live; I will lift up my hands in Thy name.
—Psalm 63:2-4

The psalmist who wrote Psalm 63 knew these feelings. He discovered the dependable and strong love of God as the anchor in his life.

✎ **How did you personally experience the steadfast love of God during a time when you felt "dry and weary"?**

_____

_____

When I remember Thee on my bed, I meditate on Thee in the night watches,
—Psalm 63:6

✎ **Have you thought about God as you lay on your bed struggling with a personal hurt or challenge?** ❏ Yes ❏ No

For Thou hast been my help, And in the shadow of Thy wings I sing for joy. My soul clings to Thee; Thy right hand upholds me... But the king will rejoice in God; Everyone who swears by Him will glory, For the mouths of those who speak lies will be stopped.
—Psalm 63:7-8, 11

✎ **If you have your Bible, read Psalm 63 in its entirety or reread the portions of the psalm from this page. Underline each word or phrase that gives an attitude or action of God. Circle the words or phrases which give an attitude or action we can have toward God.**

No matter how painful or complex the problems we face in our watches of the night, we can reach out to God for help. When life is at its worst, the situation gives God an opportunity to prove Who He is. Experiences of grief and suffering may cause us to feel we are living in a dry and weary land. We may struggle and lose sleep. But even in our darkest nights, God is wide awake and taking care of us. His right hand holds us up. No enemy, not even addiction, can conquer and destroy those of us who trust the power of God. In God's shadow, we can sing for joy. Victory is assured!

**Loving God more**

I remember a friend who never prayed without including the words, "God, help me love You more." I have since included these words regularly in my own prayers. My love for God is the energy which keeps me moving on the track of recovery. God's love surrounds me; it also fills me.

I have not always so valued God's love. Although I had given God my mind, emotions, and life, for many years I did not have a daily relationship with Him.

- If I describe God as my Boss, our relationship was one where we communicated on an occasional basis. As a result, I did not understand what He wanted of me.
- If I consider God as my Comforter, the little time we spent together meant I had to rely on my own strength.
- If I think of God as my Heavenly Father, we communicated only on Father's Day.
- If I say He is my Spiritual Head, I was without sound direction.
- If I call on God as my Spiritual Husband, we commuted long distances to meet every now and then when my schedule allowed.

In other words, my relationship with God was not complete. The potential for strength was present, because God does not let us go. But our relationship was lacking, because I failed to communicate with God regularly.

My relationship with God changed when I began to spend time regularly in Bible study, prayer, and meditation. The more I understand God, the more I love Him. The more I love Him, the more I see His work in my life. The more I see Him working, the more I want His will for my life. And this draws me back to Bible study and prayer. Regular time with God is the power in my life; I could not continue without it. I don't know how I survived as long as I did without its strength and joy.

*God does not just want you emptied of addiction; He wants you to be filled with His Spirit.*

Recovering from addiction is good—part of what God wants for your life. However, God wants more. He does not just want you emptied of addiction; He wants you to be filled with His Spirit. Abundant living is a process of growth which requires continued renewal and growing trust in God. You can no more be strong by communicating with God one time and not talking with Him again than you can eat one big meal and never get hungry again. The walk of life drains our spiritual energy and demands regular renewal. You cannot experience the blessings of the abundant life unless you spend time with God regularly.

✎ **When do you currently spend time in Bible study and/or prayer?**

_____

_____

✎ **If you are willing to commit to spending more time in spiritual growth, describe your plans to set aside the time.**

_____

_____

➤ Make a commitment to read your Bible through in one year's time. You may subscribe to *Open Windows*, a daily devotional guide that includes a Bible reading calendar by calling 1-800-458-2772.

✎ Write your personal prayer for today.

_____

_____

_____

## DAY 3

# Set and Achieve New Goals

Scott said: "When I stopped smoking cigars, I set a goal—not to smoke for six weeks. No way could I make a commitment to give up cigars for the rest of my life. That was just too far off—kind of like *forever*, and I didn't think I could make it that long. So I just didn't smoke for one-day-at-a-time. Now, I have reached my goal. It's been six weeks today that I have not used any tobacco at all. Today, I woke up and realized I had reached my goal. It's been a good six weeks—easier than I thought. I do not want to go back to where I was, so I'm setting a new goal. For as long as I can make it one-day-at-a-time, I will continue smoke-free. Hopefully, that will be the rest of my life, but all I can take care of is today."

This I recall to my mind, Therefore I have hope. The Lord's lovingkindnesses indeed never cease, For His compassions never fail. They are new every morning; Great is Thy faithfulness. "The Lord is my portion," says my soul, "Therefore I have hope in Him."
—Lamentations 3:21-24

✎ Read Lamentations 3:21-24 which appears in the margin. What does the phrase "the Lord is my portion" mean to you?

_____

_____

_____

✎ In what ways are you finding that the love of the Lord is steadfast and new every morning?

_____

_____

_____

In previous times, addiction to tobacco was your portion. It was allocated in a specific number of cigarettes or chews per day. Now, the Lord is your portion—your part of life, but your "portion" of the Lord is unlimited. This means you have a different future ahead. Think back to your first support group session. Most likely, your plans for abstinence were not very clear, and you were not sure if would be successful. Now, you have a new confidence and ability which you have acquired one day at a time. You have changed in significant ways during your action stage of recovery.

The word *action* means *effort* or *that you put forth energy*. Action usually but not always results from attitude. Sometimes you have to "act as if" and let your attitude catch up later. Sales trainers use this philosophy. They teach: "Act enthusiastic, and you will be enthusiastic." It's a good philosophy to apply to recovery.

✎ **Can you remember any times you have had to "act as if" you were doing OK, just to get through an experience?** ❑ **Yes** ❑ **No What happened?**

_____

_____

✎ **Did you later have a positive attitude about your accomplishment or a feeling of pride?** ❑ **Yes** ❑ **No In the margin explain your answer.**

## Evaluating Your Progress

Now that you are entering the Maintenance stage of recovery, don't think that you can be inactive and quit working your program. To continue planning and reaching goals is just as important now as it was on your first day of abstinence. You are either growing or regressing, moving forward or moving backward, planting or pulling up, building up or tearing down. Passive recovery does not exist—even during maintenance.

You had definite reasons for giving up tobacco. You set specific goals and made plans for how you would reach them. One of your goals might have been to give up tobacco in order to be healthier. If so, you have partially met that goal. You are now healthier than you were before you quit using tobacco. Perhaps you are able to breathe easier, cough less, or have a healthier diet. Now that you have reached part of your goal, you might wish to set new goals which will continue to make you a healthier person.

✎ **What were your reasons for giving up tobacco? Write them here.**

_____

_____

_____

✎ **Beside each reason, write *reached* if you have accomplished that goal. Write *progressed* if you made changes but will continue working on it.**

For example, perhaps one of your reasons for quitting was "To live longer with my family." You have lived longer—about eight weeks to be exact, but is this long enough, or do you wish to live even longer with your family? Most likely, you want more time with your loved ones. If so, continue or begin healthy lifestyle changes. If you have been exercising on a regular basis, do not stop. By continuing to exercise, you will be more likely to maintain abstinence from tobacco as well as reach the goal of living longer with your family. Avoid the temptation to say, *I have reached my goal of not using tobacco. I can quit working my program now and take it easy.*

### Later I felt—

_____

_____

_____

_____

### Keep working

➤ For each item marked as "progressed," continue to make specific daily or weekly plans which will allow you to continue your progress. Make a copy of the weekly plan sheet, and complete it for next week.

You can set personal goals for maintenance. Here are some suggestions—

**Set maintenance goals**

- Evaluate your progress periodically. Think about each of the four areas of personal growth: physical, psychological, interpersonal, and spiritual. Your life is balanced when you are working on positive attitudes and actions in each area.
- Continue actions which are helpful; discontinue those which are not.
- Consider making plans to attend an ongoing support group for recovering addicts. This can be a 12-Step group, or your group might decide to become an ongoing support group.
- If you begin to struggle with recovery, return to actions which were helpful during the early weeks of abstinence.
- Be part of someone else's recovery. Nothing promotes growth and change like accountability to some other person. When you give away what you have learned, you help the other person. You also strengthen your ability to remain abstinent.

✎ In the margin write this week's Scripture verse from memory. Review all the verses you have memorized during these weeks.

## DAY 4

Jesus looked at him, and said, "You are Simon the son of John; you shall be called Cephas" (which translated means Peter).
—John 1:42

# A New Name/A New Start

In Bible times, names reflected the person's identity. When a person had a profound experience or personality change, his or her name was changed. This happened to Abram whose name was changed to Abraham. Jacob's name became Israel. Sarai became Sarah. In each case, the change in name reflected a change in the person. Jesus changed Simon's name to Peter, meaning Stone or Rock, as a reflection of the strength of character Peter would later use in helping establish the early churches.

Several weeks ago you began the journey of recovery. Like the disciples, you were looking for something. Your goals may have been clear and precise, or perhaps you were not sure what it was you were looking for. Now, many weeks later, your search has brought more than you expected. Maybe all you wanted was abstinence, but you found new friends. Possibly you were looking for personal strength but found spiritual strength as you relied on Jesus in a new way. You were on a quest, a search, for a different way of daily living. You responded to an invitation to "come and see" what this support group was all about. You have changed during this time.

➤ Think about how you have changed during the past few weeks. Reflect on physical, psychological, interpersonal, and spiritual growth.

As you reflect on changes in your attitudes and actions these past weeks, you may discover that you have a stronger trust in God. You may feel more positive about your personal discipline or your example to friends and family. Most likely these changes have been evident to others who have commented to you about the changes they see. In a way, you have a new identity.

✎ By what names were you known as a child?

_____

✎ By what name(s) do your parents refer to you?

_____

✎ By what other names are you known?

_____

✎ If Jesus were to give you a new name based on changes you have made during recovery, what would it be?

_____

✎ Think about the other members in your group. What names would you give each of them based on changes you see?

_____

_____

_____

_____

_____

**Promise for change**

This "new" name reflects changes you have made and the hope of who you are becoming. It represents the goal you are working toward. The abundant life is not a static place but rather a positive attitude about life. Christ offers you the opportunity to change. He offers not just a hope or wish for change but the way and power to change. Christ provides both the goal for change and the resources necessary to reach the goal. Keep working to live up to your new name.

➤ Spend some time in prayer. Ask God to show you the identity He wants to develop in your life. Thank Him for your new "name."

## Release the Past

"My name is Judy, and I have been smoke-free for nine weeks now. This is the longest I have ever been off cigarettes. The first two weeks were terrible; I never want to go through that again. The next four weeks weren't so bad, and I feel better now. I can breathe easier, and I have started exercising. The weekly support group sessions and daily Bible reading have helped tremendously. I'm pretty confident that I will never go back to smoking, but occasionally I still have strong urges that are difficult to deal with. I'm scared because our support group is ending. I'm not ready to be on my own. I need the accountability and encouragement of a support group. The local hospital has a nicotine dependence support group, and I called and enrolled. I begin next week. To lose this group and the people who have come to mean so much to me is difficult, but I am looking forward to starting a new group."

They (Paul and Barnabas) returned... strengthening the souls of the disciples, encouraging them to continue in the faith, and saying, "Through many tribulations we must enter the kingdom of God."

—Acts 14:21-22

---

Acts chapter 14 of tells about several actions of the members of the early churches. If you read the entire chapter, you would see that they:
1. Supported each other during times of persecution and tribulation.
2. Strengthened and encouraged other believers.
3. Prayed and fasted.
4. Trusted one another to the care of God.
5. Talked about all that God had done.

In many respects, these early Christians shared their lives on a support group basis. They had many of the same attitudes and actions which your group members have experienced and shared. They talked with one another when things were not going well (tribulations and persecution) and offered encouragement. They prayed for one another and even fasted as part of their prayers. When good things happened, they shared this good news with one another. Their shared faith in God resulted in many miracles.

✎ **In the margin describe how your nicotine recovery support group has helped you.**

Being part of a support group can be a wonderful experience. Sharing grief and joy bonds members in a way that cannot be compared to any other experience. If you have never been in a group like this before, to think about losing the support of other group members may be difficult. Still, now is time to say good-bye unless your group has decided to continue. If your group continues, you are encouraged to invite other tobacco users who wish to begin recovery to join you. In either case, your group will not be the same. In spite of the deep fellowship which bonded you to one another, it is time to move on. Remember, "to everything there is a season" (Ecclesiastes 3).

You may want to think about one of three options for further growth. Through this experience you may have discovered some additional issues in your life on which you desire to work. In the last lesson you will learn about some additional resources you might want to explore. Or, you may have found that you can have a ministry to other tobacco users by facilitating another *Quitting for Good* group.

Think back on the weeks you have shared with your group. Each person has strengthened you in some way, some more than others. Reflect on each member of your group and complete the following activity.

✎ **Use a separate sheet of paper, and divide it into four columns. In the first column write the name of each person in your group, leaving a few lines between each name. Don't forget to include your facilitator(s). After each name, use the next three columns to answer each of the following questions about the impact of each person on your recovery. We have provided a sample worksheet for you at the top of the next page.**

1. **What did you learn from this person? It may have been something the person said or did or even something you observed.**

2. **Have you seen the attitudes and actions of this person change? How?**

3. **What words of encouragement do you have for this person?**

---

**My group has helped by—**

_____

_____

_____

_____

_____

---

| Name | From this person I learned— | How this person has changed— | Words of encouragement for this person— |
|---|---|---|---|
| | | | |
| | | | |
| | | | |

After you have answered the three questions about each member of your group, take time to thank God for how each member has enriched your recovery. Your final group session will be a "good-bye group." The entire time will be spent sharing thoughts on today's activities in your workbook. You will be given opportunity to share what the group has meant to you as well as what you learned from each person.

**Difficult to say good-bye**

The final session will be difficult in some ways. Saying good-bye can be difficult, especially when the other person is loved and appreciated. It may also be difficult for you to share personal feelings of gratitude as you thank and encourage your friends. Pray that you will say what God wants you to say to each person in your support group.

Above all, give God the glory for what He has done in your life. Your recovery is not due to your own efforts or those of your support group. The power of healing always comes from God, and He deserves the thanks.

# DAY
## 5

# Where Do You Go from Here?

We all need to grow. None of us has arrived. As you have worked through *Quitting for Good*, we hope that you have come to understand yourself better. We hope that you have come to understand and to love God more. We hope that you have also discovered areas in which you need to grow. You may have identified specific areas for further growth. The LIFE® Support Group Series materials are intended to assist you in any of the following areas.

Many of us struggle with weight gain or with healthy eating and exercise habits. To help you grow in developing a healthy lifestyle you may want to consider *First Place: A Christ-Centered Health Program* (Nashville: LifeWay Press). This program applies biblical insights and relevant nutritional information in a support-group process. *First Place* groups learn and practice healthful eating, exercise, and spiritual-growth habits. Member's Book, product number 7227-72; Leader's Guide, product number 7228-72.

Setting goals is an important step in all growth. As you complete *Quitting for Good*, you probably can think of additional physical, psychological, interpersonal, and spiritual growth areas.

 **Think about areas in your life in which you need to grow. In the list at the top of the next page, rank your top three priorities by writing *1* in the blank beside the subject in which you most need to grow; *2* by your second choice, and *3* by your third.**

___ Understanding the Bible        ___ Knowing God's will
___ Developing your prayer life    ___ Becoming a disciple maker
___ Building witnessing skills     ___ Conquering codependency

___ Other: _____

The facilitator's guide for *Quitting for Good* contains a list of resources you may obtain to help you to grow in one or more of these areas. You may want to ask your group facilitator to provide you a copy of that list of resources. Your group may even desire to continue to grow by having a group using one of these books.

Your group facilitator also has a page titled "Quitting for Good Participant Survey." We are asking you to help us follow up on this material by copying and returning the survey. We will use the information on this form to evaluate the effectiveness of this book and the support group format. Your honesty will give us direction in the future. You may receive a follow-up questionnaire or phone call a few months after you mail your form. Again, the intent will be to offer support and encouragement during your continued recovery progress. Your name and phone number will not be used for any other purpose and will not be given to any other group or person. All information on the form will be confidential. Thank you for your willingness to help us and future group members by completing this form and returning it to us. If we can be of help to you during the coming days of recovery, please write and let us know.

Life can be an exciting adventure. The options you have reviewed present some possibilities for a lifestyle of continued growth, health, and service.

Finally, I as writer and the members of the LIFE® Support Group Series team also wish to say good-bye. We sincerely pray that we have been faithful in offering you the direction and learning opportunities needed for your recovery. We have each personally experienced the pain and joy of recovery (although not always related to nicotine). Although we may not know you and may never see your face, we have been praying for you. We began praying for you while the idea of this Christ-centered support group for nicotine dependent people was only a dream. We will continue to pray for you.

➤ *Father, we come with grief and joy to the final prayer of this workbook. The journey has been difficult at times, but the burden has been lightened by the support of friends and the working presence of Your Holy Spirit. Thank You for Your love, and for the daily power and motivation which You have given. I ask that You continue to work in me as You complete the work of recovery begun a few weeks ago, in Jesus name. Amen.*